"In their new book, *Sustai~~n~~* ~~... and~~ Mark DeVries tackle this import ~~... far~~ surpass my expectations. Whether you've been working with young adults for decades or you're a curious church member concerned about where all the young adults went, this book is hands down one of the most accessible and practical books available on this topic today. With its winsome prose drawn from a deep pool of ministerial wisdom, *Sustainable Young Adult Ministry* will no doubt become a classic in the ever-widening swath of literature surrounding young adult spirituality and what the church must do to reengage this generation anew."

Jason Brian Santos, mission coordinator for Christian formation, Presbyterian Mission Agency

"'What do we do about young adults?' There are very few challenges facing the church today that are so regularly paired with a sense of helplessness and panic. Churches are desperate for answers, but they have mostly just given up, assuming the solution is beyond them. Hark! On the horizon! A book with genuine help, honest encouragement, and buckets full of hope. There is, quite literally, no other book that I'm aware of that provides what this book provides."

Mark Oestreicher, partner, The Youth Cartel

"Once again, DeVries and the Ministry Architects team have demystified ministry in a way that leaves us feeling less concerned with how we fit into a pair of skinny jeans and more focused on the healthy (and accessible) habits that lead to a vital culture for ministry. If your experience is anything like mine, you'll twinge at the accuracy of their common ministry mistakes, but you'll laugh enough to know that you're not alone. In the end, I had a punch list that left me feeling like effective ministry to young adults wasn't so impossible after all."

Trey Wince, director of new disciples, United Methodist Church of Greater New Jersey

"Pontier and DeVries offer an integrative and adaptive approach to relational ministry with young adults as they are, not as we wish them to be. This practical and holistic read will help your church build a young adult ministry with them instead of one for them."

Victoria White, leadership education, Duke University

"In the same winsome style of *Sustainable Youth Ministry*, this book paints a simple and challenging picture of the young adult ministry landscape. However, unlike many books I have read on this topic, Mark and Scott don't just tell us how to think but help you develop a clear plan of what to do. Whether you are a veteran youth worker or rookie ministry leader, this book provides a clear road map to navigate and succeed in young adult ministry. *Sustainable Young Adult Ministry* is sure to change the trajectory of young adult ministry for the next fifty years. I only wish I had this book five years ago."

James Wilson Jr., Freedom Life Church, Hampton, Virginia

"There are two kinds of perspectives: the *outside* perspective of the one who studies (the academic and the researcher) and the *inside* perspective of the one who experiences (the practitioner and the player). In this crucial and desperately needed book, Mark and Scott combine the strengths of both perspectives into a juggernaut case for a radical change in the way church leaders are attempting to reach a disappearing generation. Their systems approach to ministry strategy may sound, well, unsexy—but they've chosen the road less traveled, which is the path of courage. Don't just read this book; use it."

Rick Lawrence, author of *Jesus-Centered Youth Ministry, The Jesus-Centered Life,* and *The God Who Fights for You*

"I don't know of many churches that have truly cracked the code of young adult ministry, let alone the issue of sustainability. This book helps unlock the code and lays a clear path to a preferred future. Once you and your team have read it, do what the book says . . . put it down and go meet with some young adults who have so much to teach us. The future of the church depends on this."

Alex Shanks, assistant to the bishop, Florida Annual Conference of the United Methodist Church

"So many voices, academic institutions, research organizations, and denominations are sounding the alarm about the decline of young adults in church. However, very few are looking at this issue from a holistic, systemic, developmental, cultural, and common-sense perspective. Mark DeVries and Scott Pontier's *Sustainable Young Adult Ministry* is a wellspring of fresh yet sensible thinking about the spirituality and formation of emerging young adults. This book is filled with both accessible practical concepts along with thoughtful theological considerations. Instead of offering faddish and gimmicky program strategies that are too often embarrassingly inept, the authors put processes, procedures, and systems in the forefront of what it takes to curate environments of transformation. Having ministered with young adults for four decades, I highly recommend this important book, not just to youth pastors, young adult pastors, and pastors but also to all who love the church and its future."

Mike King, president/chief executive officer of Youthfront, author of *Presence-Centered Youth Ministry*

"I wish every church that wanted to build relationships with my college students would read *Sustainable Young Adult Ministry*. This book will help churches avoid mistakes that most make and develop a systemic approach to young adult ministry that works."

Teri McDowell Ott, chaplain of Monmouth College

"There are far too many easy answers thrown around these days about why 'young people' aren't in church, and they tend to be unhelpful. Mark DeVries and Scott Pontier set about the difficult task of creating a nuanced analysis of the pained relationship between young adults and the church, and take on the even more difficult task of providing meaningful recommendations about how that relationship might be restored. Their insights are helpful for anyone wanting to tap into the passion of the younger generation."

Meredith Mills, Westminster United Methodist Church, Houston

sustainable young adult ministry

making it work, making it last

Mark DeVries and Scott Pontier

An imprint of InterVarsity Press
Downers Grove, Illinois

InterVarsity Press
P.O. Box 1400, Downers Grove, IL 60515-1426
ivpress.com
email@ivpress.com

InterVarsity Press® is the book-publishing division of InterVarsity Christian Fellowship/USA®, a movement of students and faculty active on campus at hundreds of universities, colleges, and schools of nursing in the United States of America, and a member movement of the International Fellowship of Evangelical Students. For information about local and regional activities, visit intervarsity.org.

All Scripture quotations, unless otherwise indicated, are taken from The Holy Bible, New International Version®, NIV®. Copyright © 1973, 1978, 1984, 2011 by Biblica, Inc.™ Used by permission of Zondervan. All rights reserved worldwide. www.zondervan.com. The "NIV" and "New International Version" are trademarks registered in the United States Patent and Trademark Office by Biblica, Inc.™

While any stories in this book are true, some names and identifying information may have been changed to protect the privacy of individuals.

Figure 1.1. is used with permission, courtesy of the Hartford Institute.

Cover design and image composite: Faceout Studio
Interior design: Daniel van Loon
Images: stack of wooden twigs: © Hipatia / Shutterstock Images
book of matches: © Mega Pixel / Shutterstock Images
single wooden match: © Noppanun K / Shutterstock Images

ISBN 978-0-8308-4152-3 (print)
ISBN 978-0-8308-6555-0 (digital)

Printed in the United States of America ∞

InterVarsity Press is committed to ecological stewardship and to the conservation of natural resources in all our operations. This book was printed using sustainably sourced paper.

Library of Congress Cataloging-in-Publication Data
A catalog record for this book is available from the Library of Congress.

P 25 24 23 22 21 20 19 18 17 16 15 14 13 12 11 10 9 8 7 6 5 4 3 2 1

Y 37 36 35 34 33 32 31 30 29 28 27 26 25 24 23 22 21 20 19

Scott

To Travis Radaz, my young adult partner—
a living, breathing test subject and dear
friend. Indeed, he's the clearest example
I know who shows how young adults are
changing the world.

Mark

To Leigh DeVries, my wise, gifted, and
discerning daughter, who seldom met an idea
she wasn't passionate about.

Contents

Introduction 1

1 How Do You Solve a Problem Like Young Adults?
A Ruthlessly Honest Snapshot of the State
of Today's Young Adult Ministry 9

2 Mistake 1: Learn About Young Adults. 21

3 Mistake 2: Change the Worship Style. 35

4 Mistake 3: Expect the Youth Director to Do It 44

5 Mistake 4: Start by Creating
a Young Adult Program. 55

6 Mistake 5: Wait Until They're Ready. 64

7 Mistake 6: Give Up Too Soon. 75

8 Beyond Fixing 85

9 Paradox 1: Succeed by Being Willing to Fail 91

10 Paradox 2: Focus on Young Adults
by Taking the Focus off Young Adults. 106

11 Paradox 3: Reach Young People
by Gathering More Old People 115

12 Paradox 4: Reach One Young Adult at a Time
Through a System to Reach Them All 128

13 Paradox 5: Respond to Lack of Commitment
by Asking for More 139

14 Paradox 6: Attract Young Adults to Your
Church by Sending Them Away   151

15 I Don't Know . . . Yet: Practicing the
Long Obedience   164

16 Failure Isn't an Option—It's a Certainty   180

Acknowledgments   191

Discussion Questions   194

Appendix: The Young Adult Ministry Road Map   202

Notes   207

Additional Resources   215

Introduction

Success has always been a great liar.

FRIEDRICH NIETZSCHE

Young adult ministry to me feels like a big mystery.
Most of the questions I ask don't have any answers.

DAVID, A YOUNG ADULT WHO LEADS
A YOUNG ADULT MINISTRY

W e had done it.

In just a few short years, we had achieved what the other, older churches in our city had never experienced: we had young adults!

On any given week, in fact, 50 to 60 percent of our attendees were *under* the age of thirty.

We had a hip, young worship leader: a twenty-one-year-old guitar player with amazing skills and irrepressible charisma. He led a band that wrote its own music, produced its own album, and certainly never seemed to play a worship song that was more than eighteen months old.

Rock Harbor Church was drawing in young adults with a completely nontraditional experience. Our worship space looked like a warehouse. I preached in jeans and an untucked shirt from behind a table, not a pulpit. We didn't take ourselves too seriously, and college students and twenty-somethings connected naturally with a climate of authenticity—the exact opposite of the ostentatiousness they'd come to expect from church.

Prior to becoming the pastor at Rock Harbor, I served in youth ministry for fifteen years, both in the local church and through Young Life. As a youth pastor, one of the saddest times of the year was graduation season, when our core seniors left the program.

Just about the time young people were beginning to get their leadership legs, they were heading out!

Leading a congregation like Rock Harbor gave me the chance to offer young adults ongoing leadership roles in the church. In our congregation, college students served in key positions, and our leadership team was peppered with twenty-somethings. Young adults regularly invited others to worship, welcomed friends into a relationship with Christ, and volunteered in our community.

I was thrilled to lead a young adult congregation. As a church, Rock Harbor embodied so much about the young adult experience:

* We were a "church within a church," worshiping inside a parent church in a separate auditorium (translation: old enough to move out of our parents' basement but not quite able to do so).

* We still relied on our parent church to cover our financial costs, which, of course, they were happy to do.

But we were accomplishing what many had tried and very few had actually done: we were thriving in our ministry with young adults.

It felt incredibly energizing to pastor a brand-new church, reaching the very demographic that experts said simply wasn't interested in church. Anything felt possible. The congregation was willing to try anything, and people were energized by the momentum of change. It was the opportunity of a lifetime, the chance to live the dream God had placed on my heart, a dream you may be dreaming as well.

By now, you've probably noticed the past tense in much of my story.

Five years after opening, Rock Harbor Church closed.

In Search of Sustainable Young Adult Ministry

We had plenty of reasons for closing the church that had nothing to do with young adults. Being physically located within a larger church provided a host of challenges related to identity. Were we an additional worship service? A separate church?

With all the energy and enthusiasm around worship, we struggled to maintain a vision beyond the Sunday morning worship experience. And our worship space was too small for a critical mass to grow.

Some reasons for the closure related directly to the unique dynamics of creating a church focused on young adults, not the least of which was finances. Young adults just don't have access to as much money as churchgoers twice their age, and their giving patterns are much more diffuse and less institutional than the generations who came before them.

Building a sustainable budget proved impossible when such a significant portion of our congregation lived on ramen noodles in dorm rooms. At one point I even took another role in our multisite church to keep my salary out of our congregation's budget. I would lend my preaching each week, but leading the congregation could no longer be my primary responsibility.

We were dealing, by definition, with a transient population. Though our overall attendance stayed almost exactly the same for the final three years, congregational "membership" turned over almost entirely during that same time frame. As a result, we had a lot of new visitors but very few owners of the church's mission and ministry.

One month we'd have an entire group of college students who loved everything about our church; the next month we'd discover that same group had moved to another church in town because someone in the group started dating someone from *that* church. Although we didn't have difficulty attracting new faces, at times it felt like trying to scoop water with a butterfly net. We just couldn't gain traction.

After adding up all those pieces, we realized our church couldn't sustain ministry any longer in its current form. We considered merging with another campus in our multisite church, but the opportunities just didn't align. We considered moving to another location or hiring another pastor to take the church into the next phase of life, but the financial cost was simply too high.

After much discernment and prayer, we realized a couple of things. First, we knew God wanted us to be "sent." We weren't sure how or where, but we realized the DNA of this church was important and God didn't want it to be lost. Second, we had no single option in front of us to do that. Luke 14:33 was always close in our prayers in those days: "In the same way, those of you who do not give up everything you have cannot be my disciples."

At that stuck moment, we were one of the coolest, hippest churches in town, reaching the demographic Holy Grail, yet we were unable to continue the church without some kind of intervention. I hoped we might experience the church version of the hero narrative, with someone showing up in the nick of time with an answer—a building or a big, anonymous check in the mail.

Instead, I stood before my congregation and announced we'd be closing our church in six weeks. That's a sermon I never want to preach again.

I hope you never have to preach it either.

The Tumbleweed Diaspora

In hindsight, I see a bit more clearly some of the crucial mistakes we made in our ministry with young adults and college students. And unfortunately, I see the vast majority of churches doing almost exactly the same things.

These mistakes are easy to make because they look so smart, so innovative, so exciting. But they simply don't work in the long run. The thing about mistakes is they often don't *look* like mistakes when you're making them. In fact, they often look like success. Young adult ministries that launch and consequently fizzle may be the single most common narrative for this kind of work in churches.

One unintended consequence of our church's closing was the fruitful sending of young adults to serve and lead in other ministries and churches. As a congregation, we began to identify closely with the tumbleweed.

You may not know that tumbleweeds begin as *green* plants that grow in the ground until it's time to reproduce. When that time comes, they draw all their moisture and nutrients into the seeds at their core, turning the rest brittle, dry, and essentially dead. Eventually, the plant breaks off at its stem, and the wind blows it away.

This is when tumbleweeds turn into that bundle of thistles blowing between the good guy and the villain at high noon in old Westerns. But here's the fascinating thing: everywhere a tumbleweed bounces, it leaves seeds behind to grow a new plant, spreading life wherever it rolls.

The Rock Harbor story is a tumbleweed story—one that, thankfully, isn't finished. Our unintentional experiment with becoming a tumbleweed church continues to plant the seeds of passionate young Christians wherever it bounces, creating a veritable tumbleweed diaspora.

Yes, there's deep sadness that our story ended as it did, one and done. I wish we could have become more of a tumbleweed greenhouse, repeating the process over and over again, multiplying seeds for many more years. But the mistakes we made from the very beginning set us up as unsustainable.

I write this book during the first years of planting a new church. So far, it's been an amazing ride, but I know we're just getting started. All our past mistakes were only compost for our ministry's next chapter—and now hopefully for yours, as well.

Leaving the Harbor

As you read this book, I hope you'll become convinced, as I am, that ministry with young adults is within the reach of every church in America. It is not the exclusive responsibility of new, hip (and too often short-lived) churches. Through trial and error, accident and providence, we've stumbled onto a few principles for working with young adults that almost every church can adapt and apply.

If you're not already, I hope that by the end of this book you'll be convinced that if we miss out on reaching this generation, we'll have missed the opportunity of a lifetime. I hope you'll become even more convinced that a church like yours can seize this specific moment in history and pass the baton to the next generation by working a deliberate, sustainable process where the gospel flourishes among young adults.

And if you find yourself running headlong into ministry with young adults and college students, if you have the greatest ideas about reaching the next generation in unique and amazing ways, I hope you'll pause. As Otto von Bismarck famously said, "Only a fool learns from his own mistakes. The wise [person] learns from the mistakes of others."

My invitation, then, is for you to not just push the pause button but to know the landscape of other people's previous mistakes before you catapult headlong into young adult ministry with the same disappointing results.

Style Decisions

Before launching into the meat of this book, a few explanatory notes are in order.

About names. I share lots of stories based on my conversations and ministry experiences. I decided to change the names in every story, and when it felt necessary, I changed a few details to protect people whose story I'm telling.

On the use of "I" versus "we." Although this book has been a partnership from start to finish between me, Scott Pontier, and my coauthor, Mark DeVries, we decided to write it almost entirely in the first-person singular. Here's why: though we may periodically use *we* or *our* (as I just did), we've always imagined this book as a conversation. So we've crafted it deliberately as a conversation between you, the reader, and Scott, the coach, pastor, and young adult ministry consultant. But rest assured, Mark's annoying compulsion for clarity is evident on every page!

As we begin, imagine it's just the two of us sitting across a table dreaming about how to succeed with young adults.

So grab a cup of coffee, and let's get started!

1

How Do You Solve a Problem Like Young Adults?

A Ruthlessly Honest Snapshot of the State of Today's Young Adult Ministry

> *The lowest ebb is the turn of the tide.*
>
> HENRY WADSWORTH LONGFELLOW

> *There is always a well-known solution to every human problem—neat, plausible, and wrong.*
>
> H. L. MENCKEN

There's little doubt that the American church's ministry to young adults has reached an all-time low. The next generation is in a mass exodus from the church.

An avalanche of worrisome statistics has begun to feel normal:

* "The ages of eighteen to twenty-nine are the black hole of church attendance; this age segment is 'missing in action' from most

congregations. . . . These numbers represent about eight million twentysomethings who were active churchgoers as teenagers but who will no longer be particularly engaged in a church by their thirtieth birthday."[1]

* Seventy percent of eighteen- to thirty-year-olds "who went to church regularly in high school said they quit attending by age 23."[2]

* Only 20 percent of twenty-somethings report that they "have maintained a level of spiritual activity consistent with their teenage experiences." Another 19 percent "were never significantly reached by a Christian community of faith during their teen" years.[3]

* While the number of Americans who say they have "no religion" has more than doubled since 1990,[4] "a third of adults under 30 . . . are religiously unaffiliated today, the highest percentages ever in Pew Research Center polling."[5]

* Two-thirds (67 percent) of young adults who were raised un-affiliated are still unaffiliated, a higher retention rate than most other major religious groups—and much higher than for older generations of "nones."[6]

The average church today has demonstrated clearly that it is ill-equipped to engage this generation and leverage its leadership in the life of the church. Though the challenges of reaching eighteen- to thirty-year-olds (college students and young adults) isn't a new topic for the church, the challenge of reaching young adults— eighteen- to thirty-year-olds of *this* generation—is something new.

In his book *You Lost Me*, David Kinnaman quotes an entre-preneur who works with young adults: "This next generation is not just slightly different from the past. I believe they are *discontinu-ously different* than anything we have seen before."[7]

Sure, there's a certain sameness about the challenges of ministry. It's been difficult in the past and will be difficult in the future. But now many people are realizing that this generation is unlike any that has come before.

It shouldn't be surprising, then, that churches (those that haven't given up) are struggling desperately to crack the code on engaging and retaining young adults. With few of the old tricks working, the old rules don't seem to apply. This population has fundamentally different assumptions, worldviews, and paradoxes from previous generations.

Getting Beyond Normal

Don't get me wrong: churches and ministry leaders are having lots of fine *discussions* about young adults. Typically, not a week goes by without a report somewhere about the topic of "Christianity and young adults," the first generation raised from the technological cradle.

A longtime associate pastor at a large church offers this picture of how churches can easily spend many hours, sometimes years, in passionate conversation about young adults without doing much of anything:

> I remember sitting in a church staff meeting recently with fifteen otherwise very intelligent people, eight of whom had master's or doctorates. We spent 30 or so minutes, with five or six of them dissecting with articulate passion the question of why young adults don't come to church and what "the church" should do about it.
>
> The crazy thing is, no one at the table, no one, had any positional responsibility to actually do anything. Eventually, I couldn't take it anymore.
>
> I asked, "I'm just wondering, is there anyone around the table who's going to do anything about the problems we've been discussing? How about we answer that question, and if

the answer is no, can we talk about something we'll actually do something about?"

If you've been around many church meetings, you know what happened next. I had just volunteered (happily by the way) to prepare a proposal for young adult ministry.[8]

Today's "normal" in the church is *talking* about young adult ministry and trying harder at doing what hasn't worked. Blogs, tweets, status updates, online videos, and books all seem to have coalesced into a great ecclesial handwringing. Expert prognostication abounds for why young adults and the church aren't getting along. Everyone seems to have a theory:

* Maybe it's our worship style. We're too boring.

* We're just not deep enough.

* We're failing at reaching them with their language—technology.

Arguments rage about whether we're catering to young adults too much or not enough. Sound bites, statistics, and talk-show blurbs all generate interesting conversation but not much else. Talking may be all that most churches are doing to reach young adults. And, like my friend in his staff meeting, I don't find these discussions particularly helpful.

Though solid studies of young adult *ministry* are pretty hard to find, the available ones indicate that fewer than 10 percent of churches place significant emphasis on young adult ministry at all.[9] In fact, when we contacted denominational offices about what they're doing with young adults, it wasn't uncommon to hear responses such as "We don't have those stats right now. We're working on mapping campus ministries and young adult ministries but are still in the process of collecting that data."

Although most churches are avoiding young adults altogether, a few *are* working hard to crack the young adult code, and that's good news. Sort of.

Unfortunately, like blind ferrets, these ministries are typified by reactive, frantic programming with little in the way of a proven plan. Desperate to win back this lagging generation, these churches throw money, staff, facilities, almost anything against the wall in hopes that something will stick—and quickly.

Better logos, social media strategies, and a new service project or worship style are often desperate, disconnected reactions to the problem of young adults. Sadly, frantic and desperate is almost never the quickest route to the desired results.

Thinking beyond the local church for a second, we must acknowledge that a huge cost comes with our normal way of doing young adult ministry:

* We miss out on the largest generation in history.

* We miss out on a generation with the potential to breathe life and vitality into waning congregations.

* We pass up an unparalleled opportunity to work with this generation to demonstrate the kingdom of God.

Most conversations portray young adults as the harbinger of the church's downfall, but I'm crazy enough to suggest instead that today's young adults might be the harbinger of hope for the church.

Everywhere we look, young adults are thinking about and living into ways of bettering the world. Even the way they *eat* is better for the environment. Young Christians are eager to engage with Christ *and* community. And non-Christians in the young adult ranks are acutely interested in spiritual conversations and in partnering with communities that make the world a better place.

This book is based on one bit of good news we're absolutely convinced is true: *building a thriving, sustainable young adult ministry is completely possible, and it might just change the world.*

But not if we choose to remain "normal."

Seven Simple Steps to Failure

While working with churches in their young adult ministries throughout the years, we've noticed commonalities. Here's the process they've almost all experienced before deciding to do *something* to reach young adults (see if it sounds familiar):

Step 1: People start to notice "Our church is aging."

Step 2: People start to wonder, "Why do our high-school students graduate and never come back?"

Step 3: People realize that without young adults the church will be out of business in a generation or so.

Step 4: People rail against the problems they see in the young adults they know: "They don't value the church." "They don't want to volunteer." "They don't tithe." "We just can't count on them!"

Step 5: An advice-fest ensues, with suggestions almost always beginning with "If we just . . ."

If we just have more young adults on Sundays . . .

If we just get our college students to come back when they graduate . . .

If we just reach out to the local college campus . . .

If we just change our worship style . . .

If we just have pizza after the service . . .

Step 6: Once the outcry becomes great enough to reach the ears of the senior pastor or leadership team, the decision is made: "We have to do *something* to reach young adults."

Step 7: The church or senior pastor acts. They look for someone who has the most influence and skill dealing with this demographic. They bring in the church's youth worker (or former youth worker or someone who looks like a youth worker) to begin something like a "college and career" program, usually in addition to their full-time job.

This isn't the only possibility, of course. A wide variety of other poorly thought out, oversimplified approaches exist. But this, by far, is my favorite—and the one I've seen most often.

Can we all agree it's time to get off the conveyor belt of what "normal" churches have always done? The solution to the young adult problem is *not* another meeting.

Few approaches are more common in young adult ministry than creating a study, a fellowship group, or an event that older adults believe will appeal to young adults. Seldom are these attempts more than polishing up youth group programming—a Sunday morning class, a small group, a trip here or there, maybe even a worship service of their own. We assume we're being innovative by arranging focus groups to ask young adults what kinds of programs they'd like the church to have for them!

The results prove that this approach is misdirected and misinformed. Doing what comes naturally, what feels normal, just won't work for creating a thriving young adult ministry.

Unless we fundamentally change our approach, the average church will work harder and harder, invest more and more dollars, yet have little or nothing to show for its efforts. We've discovered that the typical church makes many very predictable mistakes when attempting to build a young adult ministry.

These mistakes are so common because they seem good and logical. They aren't too complex and are often easy to implement. And they aren't far from the kind of ministry we already know how to do. Honestly, if it weren't so tragic, it would be entertaining.

The next six chapters introduce these mistakes. By the time you read them, hopefully you'll agree that none of these mistakes holds the key to building a thriving young adult ministry.

Six Young Adult Ministry Mistakes

Mistake 1. Learn about young adults. Young adults today are unique enough from previous generations that it's almost as if they speak a different language. We won't get anywhere if we start our thinking with "when I was their age . . ." It's vitally important to take time to understand the demographic we're attempting to reach. However, churches make the mistake of simply learning *about* young adults by reading books, blog posts, and survey results without building any significant relationships *with* young adults. This generation is filled with paradox and unpredictability. The only chance we have to really understand young adults is to tilt the balance dramatically in favor of getting to know them *personally*, not simply learning about them abstractly.

Mistake 2. Change the worship style. Perhaps the most common and obvious mistake in building a ministry to young adults is launching a brand-new (often called "contemporary") worship service. This is a terrible place to start. The process usually involves a church spending more money than it has but less than it needs to create a third-rate imitation of churches that have had this kind of worship in their DNA from the start. It's true that in most cities young adults flock to a church or two (usually those less than ten years old) with excellent contemporary worship. But it's a massive mistake for the average, established church to start a new service while assuming that such a change will make young adults flock to it.

Mistake 3. Expect the youth director to do it. Youth workers are great people. They're also typically extraordinarily busy. It's misdirected and seldom effective to assume that working with teenagers is the same as working with young adults. This approach may seem simple and economical, but it's the *quickest* way to underresource a ministry that almost always requires a concentrated strategy to succeed. If you want to do ministry "on the cheap," go ahead and start with the youth worker. If you want to establish a long-lasting ministry with young adults, start someplace else.

Mistake 4. Start by creating a young adult program. Young adults everywhere are asking for depth, diversity, impact, and authentic faith. What they *aren't* looking for is a group of baby boomers to plan their social events and offer spiritually focused lessons and speeches. Creating age-segregated, consumer-based experiences and calling it a young adult program is sure to keep your church in a spin cycle of disappointment. Young adults possess deep passion and are ready to engage the church and community. On a related note, asking young adults to sit in a room with other young adults and answer questions about what programs they'd like the church to provide almost never works.

Mistake 5. Wait until they're ready. Most churches place young adults in a leadership holding tank, expecting them to wait until they've paid their dues (translation: sat in the pew for a decade or more). We give lots of lip service to the need for developing emerging leaders, but frankly, most churches have absolutely no process (and no ideas) for integrating young adults into the fabric of the church, let alone into its leadership. Meanwhile, young adults lead in our culture with unprecedented entrepreneurial zeal. Most have stopped wondering why the church won't give them a seat at the grown-ups table and instead have found places to invest outside the church.

Mistake 6: Give up too soon. When it comes to designing and developing ministry for this generation, the church is just getting started. As a whole, we're still in the season of experimentation and discovery, and too many churches have already called it quits. Stymied and mystified by the challenges of this generation, the church is equally paralyzed by the requirement of change that might feel too painful to endure. After a few reactive attempts, many churches sit back and declare "We simply can't do it." And so they do nothing. But as for a woman in labor, new life comes with contractions and pain.

A Matter of Priorities

When young adult ministry does work, it can be a huge win for the church. The Hartford Institute for Religion Research and

Leadership Network reports the more intentional a church is about young adults, the bigger the percentage of young adults will be in the church (see fig. 1.1).

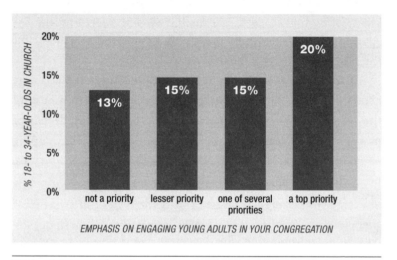

Figure 1.1. Increasing the percentage of young adults in church. *Source:* 2015 Megachurch Survey by Hartford Institute for Religion Research and Leadership Network.

It all starts with deciding that ministry to this generation is a priority. Research shows that the more emphasis churches put on young adults, the more young adults they reach. It's not that young adults are unreachable but that they haven't been anywhere near the top of the priority list for most churches. The correlation between the church's emphasis on this generation and their participation in the church can't be ignored.

And so the next generation has become a crisis on the church's doorstep. We're confused by them, confounded by them, frustrated by them, and too often willing to give up on them.

Princeton University professor Robert Wuthnow offers the church this challenge: "My view is that congregations can survive, but only if religious leaders roll up their sleeves and pay considerably more attention to young adults than they have been."[10] Paying attention requires that we treat young adults as they are, *not as we wish them to be*. It requires an investment not simply of time, money, and energy but also of experimentation and adaptation of our current models to faithfully steward the gift of young adults to our congregations today and for the future.

This book offers a measured, systems-based approach to reaching the generation that's staying away from the church in record numbers. I know: when you read "a measured, systems-based approach," you want to hit the snooze bar, right? Here's why you shouldn't.

Every single church has a calling to reach this generation. But working haphazardly, working normally won't cut it. It's time for a game plan that works not just for the isolated megachurch or new church plant but for the average, everyday, garden-variety church— the kind that's anything but trendy and hip.

A measured, systems-based approach to reaching young adults may at first seem uninspiring in the same way blocking and tackling drills are boring for football players, the way scales are boring for musicians, the way running and weight training are boring for athletes. But if churches are willing to work a clear, deliberate process, the end game can be nothing short of staggering in its impact.

The next six chapters help churches stop making the most common, most damaging mistakes simply by naming them and unmasking why these approaches almost never work. Chapter eight turns the corner to what the church *can* do. Then we'll walk through the process of building a long-term, thriving, sustainable young adult ministry in your own context.

George Bernard Shaw said, "Few people think more than two or three times a year; I have made an international reputation for myself by thinking once or twice a week."

This book is an invitation for churches to stop reacting and begin thinking in deeper, more intentional ways about this "problem" generation, pointing instead to the gifts young adults offer. Just maybe, with them, we can overcome some of the deepest challenges facing today's church.

Now let's get started.

Mistake 1

Learn About Young Adults

> *Any fool can know. The point is to understand.*
>
> ALBERT EINSTEIN

> *Hi, I'm a millennial, and I am a monster.*
>
> KELLY WILLIAMS BROWN, TEDx PRESENTATION

I magine waking up tomorrow morning, turning on the local news for the weather forecast, and hearing "Hodie tempestas 80s serenum erit medium in magno." After breakfast, you grab your shopping list as you head out the door and read something in an undecipherable alphabet.

You'll likely have no idea how to dress for the day or what to pick up at the store even though the message is clearly written—right there in black and white.

There's a good chance you don't happen to read or understand Latin or Old Norse (which is quite the gap in your education!). You likely read only English and maybe a few words of Spanish or French you remember from high school.

Many churches intuitively know that the young adult generation is speaking a markedly different language when it comes to church. Some churches have become fluent in the young adult tongue—buying books, reading blogs, and going to seminars about this language.

That's a mistake—at least as a starting point.

Any church hoping to build sustainable young adult ministry can't afford to make assumptions about what "all young adults are like." They can't afford to draw on their own dead language—based on their personal experience of "when I was their age"—to craft a picture of young adults today. They can't simply study their way to understanding young adults.

Few people become fluent in a language from a seminar or book. Fluency comes from actually being *with* native speakers.

Beyond Here

You undoubtedly learned in elementary school about all the great explorers: Columbus, Magellan, Lewis and Clark. It was exciting to imagine their bravery (and sheer lunacy!).

But for today's elementary students, another date exists on the timeline of turning points in exploration history: February 8, 2005, the day Google Maps was announced. It changed the modern world forever by placing exploration at the fingertips of anyone with an internet connection.

Since then, Google has produced countless iterations to its maps application, including satellite, terrain, and traffic views, as well as applications such as Google Moon, Mars, and Sky. Suddenly, seeing what it's actually like to sail the ocean blue (and beyond) is a realistic possibility for us all.

But maps can be tricky. Sure, they tell us what is known, understood, and cataloged. They tell us where to go and how to get there. But by design, they also tell us what we *don't* know.

Centuries ago, cartographers dramatically illustrated the vast, uncharted seas with dragons, sea serpents, and other mythical creatures, often with the words "Beyond here, there be dragons."

In a 2014 TEDx Talk, Kelly Williams Brown introduced herself by saying, "Hi, I'm a millennial, and I am a monster" (not a dragon, but mighty close).[1]

Those responsible for the cartography of young adult ministry know there's so much uncharted territory in this field, so much yet to be mapped. It would be easy to take a "Beyond here, there be dragons" approach, as far too many churches do, and view these unknowable creatures as monsters.

On church maps, we're all too familiar with the typography of classes, groups, studies, and events. And most churches have assumed that every problem can be solved using one of these common responses.

If the church is to have any hope of reaching young adults in a new territory, we must begin stepping beyond the landscape of what we already know, beyond the comfort of the well-worn programmatic maps we've used for at least the last century or so.

What We Do Know

Let's start with what we *do* know about the gap between young adults and just about everyone else. According to many experts, the next generation is unlike any that has come before it. *Discovery News* reports, "The reality is that [the differences] run much deeper . . . and may signal a shifting culture."[2]

It's easy, though, for the rest of us to understand young adults from our perspective as tourists in their world, as visitors in their zoo, seeing them only in caricature. We've grown comfortable with sweeping summary statements such as "They're texting all the time!" and "They're unbelievably entitled."

We know millennials have now replaced baby boomers as the largest generation in American history. But it's been much easier to give definition to the baby boomers or even Generation Xers than to millennials.

Millennials is one of many terms experts have used for this generation of young adults. Some use mosaics, some Generation Y, others Generation Next or the Boomerang Generation (because they so habitually leave home only to return again). Still others call them the Internet Generation because they and the World Wide Web grew up at roughly the same time.

Even millennials' age range is hard to define. Some consider eighteen to thirty the young adult years. Some use twenty-somethings, while others lump eighteen- to forty-three-year-olds together into this single generational category. Some sources use the birth-year range 1984 to 2002, or possibly 1977 to 1995. For simplicity, I use the easier-to-remember "born roughly between 1980 and 2000."

Like the individuals of this generation, millennials as a whole tend to resist easy categorization. They may be most alike in their vast differences from one another. Many—though not all—vehemently resist anything that feels like labeling or typecasting.

To offer some context, it's helpful to see millennials against the patterned backdrop of American generations in the century before them. In *Millennials Rising: The Next Great Generation*, Neil Howe and William Strauss present a fascinating side-by-side comparison of the generations. Here's a summary:

The *Greatest Generation* (or G.I. Generation, for its role in World War II) numbered about 35.2 million people. They came through the Great Depression and were foundational in the formation of modern America. Born from 1900 to 1924, this group lived through most of the twentieth century, experiencing the advent of everything from automobiles and television to personal computers and smartphones.

The *Silent Generation* (also called Traditionalists), born between 1925 and 1945, numbered about 50 million. They grew up in the shadow of the Great Depression and McCarthyism. The combination resulted in an identity of caution and withdrawal. In 1951, a *Time* magazine article used the term *Silent Generation* to refer to people born during this time frame. The name stuck, owing in part, at least, to the lack of a single, vocal leader (or US president) coming from that generation.

The *baby boomers* were the first to be born post-World War II, from 1945 to 1965. They were named for the explosive growth in US birthrates, numbering approximately 80 million (more than double the Greatest Generation). Boomers were by and large raised by stay-at-home moms typically much younger than the mothers of millennials. They experienced the Vietnam War and Woodstock, developing a mistrust of authority characterized in the iconic slogan "Never trust anyone over thirty." Baby boomers' fierce independence from their parents' generation contributed to their high-flying affluence and materialism in the 1980s. Until the millennials arrived on the scene, boomers held the record for the largest generation in US history.

Generation X has about 40 million members (about half the number of baby boomers) and generally includes people born from 1960 to 1980. The term captures this generation's antiestablishment ideology. Gen-Xers grew up wary of the dominant boomer culture and as a result created a variety of underground subcultures. Individualistic to the core, they exhibited a general pessimism about the world and a deep mistrust of government. Their negative worldview earned them the label "Slacker Generation." Gen-Xers' antiestablishment thread showed up in trends such as skateboarding and punk-rock cultures.

The final generation of adults in today's America is the *millennials,* comprising a record-breaking 89 million people. They're a paradoxical bunch, with both an unapologetic narcissism and a passionate civic-mindedness. They want to consume all the world has to offer *and* make it a better place. Having experienced both Iraq wars, they've grown up with a global mindset, made possible by their perpetual connection through technology. The internet has been a foundational metaphor (and reality) for defining how young adults understand the world and interact with it and each other. They are multitasking entrepreneurs, having been raised by helicopter parents in ways unprecedented from other generations.

Millennials, in general, distrust and are suspicious of organized religion. They tend to be moral relativists, and the cultural narrative of limitless options has created for them unprecedented identity crises.

At the same time, millennials often seek mentors from older generations. They are marrying less often and creating families later but building communities earlier. They're driven toward a customized, individualistic approach to their world yet desire deep connections with people around them. Millennials are hopeful and optimistic, in part because so many options are available to them.

Enough of the broad brush. It's time to actually *meet* a real young adult.

Meet Charlie

Charlie was born in 1982. At the beginning of the millennium, he started college. He moved into a dorm and later into an apartment with friends. He dated, held a series of jobs, and completed his degree in four and a half years.

During the summers and in between semesters, Charlie worked at a Christian camp, sensing a clear calling to full-time ministry. After college he became a youth pastor.

So far, so normal.

By traditional standards of adulthood, you'd expect that by Charlie's thirtieth birthday, he would have

1. finished school

2. moved out of the home

3. become financially independent

4. gotten married, and

5. had a first child.

But Charlie was zero for five.

In 1960, an estimated 77 percent of women and 65 percent of men had passed *all five* of these markers by age thirty. By 2000, fewer than half of women and only one-third of men—including Charlie—had completed these tasks by age thirty.[3]

This list of tasks to become an adult has been the agreed-on standard for many generations. But young adults today barely recognize it.

Instead, the Clark University "Established Adult" poll from 2014 found that the top-three markers for adulthood are:

* Accepting responsibility for oneself.

* Living financially independent.

* Making independent decisions.[4]

Not only are young adults achieving adulthood later in life, but the language they use to describe adulthood is changing as well. Here's how the *New York Times Magazine* paints the shift (with an admittedly broad brush):

> It's happening all over, in all sorts of families, not just young people moving back home but also young people taking longer to reach adulthood overall. It's a development that pre-dates the current economic doldrums, and no one knows yet what the impact will be—on the prospects of the young men

and women; on the parents on whom so many of them depend; on society, built on the expectation of an orderly progression in which kids finish school, grow up, start careers, make a family, and eventually retire to live on pensions supported by the next crop of kids who finish school, grow up, start careers, make a family, and on and on.

The traditional cycle seems to have gone off course, as young people remain untethered to romantic partners or to permanent homes, going back to school for lack of better options, traveling, avoiding commitments, competing ferociously for unpaid internships or temporary (and often grueling) Teach for America jobs, forestalling the beginning of adult life.[5]

Charlie is just living out the new normal for young adults, right? Around age thirty, he moved back in with his parents, leaving the world of full-time work to pursue a graduate degree.

But if you took time to actually have a conversation with Charlie, you'd learn he isn't *choosing* to wander or to delay moving into adulthood. He'd be quick to tell you it's not like he *decided* not to get married. In fact, he says, he desperately *wants* to be married and is actually a little nervous he won't find someone.

Charlie would explain that his church became strapped for cash in an economic downturn and was about to eliminate his position. Considering the lack of alternatives, heading back to school was a good option. He'd let you know he wanted to buy a house but couldn't qualify for a mortgage in a neighborhood he'd like to live in.

From Charlie, you'd learn that the trends don't fully reflect reality for young adults and how they move through the world.

The Explorers Method

The successful explorers of old didn't have complicated approaches. Their basic method often boiled down to "just keep going." That isn't a bad starting point for charting our own way through the new territory of young adult ministry.

Being successful explorers in this field requires that we follow the lead of Dory of *Finding Nemo* and "just keep swimming," moving (respectfully) into young adults' lives and letting them impact ours as well. We have to begin building actual relationships with them. We do have an advantage, though, that people working with young adults in previous generations didn't: young adults are deeply interested in connecting with other generations. They may seem disinterested in the church, but they aren't disinterested in people like you. They're eager for older generations to take steps toward them rather than simply observing from a distance.

Here's what Angela discovered.

Angela is in her midfifties, with two sons, one almost done with college and the other soon to have his first child. She's passionate about her faith and her church, leading Bible studies, starting women's ministries, and leading the missions committee.

Angela had every reason to claim a full plate. But recently she started helping with her church's new ministry for young adults. To gather information, Angela thought it would be helpful to visit the college campus. "That was my first mistake," she says with a laugh.

She now frequents the campus for lunch or coffee meetings and mentors a group of young women in their twenties. Angela even got a membership to the university's athletic facility and does her daily workouts right next to students. In fact, she met Jenny running on a treadmill.

After seeing Jenny a couple of times, Angela struck up a conversation. Eventually, that conversation revealed Jenny's passion to become a missionary and a desire to engage that passion more in her life. Angela invited her to church, and soon afterward Jenny actually joined the church's mission team and began providing a voice for college students in the church's leadership.

All that happened because Angela chose to live *inside* the young adult world rather than expecting young adults to show up at church because of a new contemporary service or a Facebook account.

Beyond Today's Map

When we rely on articles, newscasts, headlines, and books (including this one) to inform our map of young adult ministry, "learning about young adults" is really "making assumptions about young adults."

Even churches that study the problem of young adult ministry quickly place them into known categories, assuming that their development and engagement will (and should!) follow more or less the same road map that previous generations traversed.

You can hear the assumption in comments such as:

* Sure, they'll go away for a while during college, but when they have that first baby, they'll be back in church.

* I did the same thing—most of us did—taking time away from church when we left for college.

These mistaken perceptions are predicated on the idea that of course this population will come back as soon as they start having children. This mistake excuses our neglect with the blind confidence that, if we do nothing, young adults will be back. It's a way of staying paralyzed with inaction.

Therefore, one of the first signs that a church is actually ready to do young adult ministry is when leadership finally realizes, "They ain't comin' back."

Unfortunately, the natural next step is to study *about* young adults, usually in circular, anxious conversations. We read a few trends, watch a few YouTube videos and TED Talks, read a book or two, and then implement simplistic solutions using the exact same categories we used with previous generations. We travel the well-worn path of programs, studies, and events even when those paths are leading us in exactly the wrong direction.

Travis helped me see this mistake for what it is.

Meet Travis

You can learn a lot about frogs by dissecting them in biology class. You can pin them down, cut them open, and learn all about their organs and biology. But you'll never really *know* the frog's life— its favorite lily pad, its favorite fly, or what time of day it loves to sit in the sun. To know those kinds of things, you'll need to learn in an entirely different way.

Travis was my frog. He embodied so many young adult stereotypes. At the time of this writing, he's in his midtwenties and recently married. He doesn't plan to have kids anytime soon and never made it through college.

I met Travis when he was nineteen. He'd dropped out of college after a single semester. He had tried to do "what he was supposed to do," get a degree and become a real adult. But he said it just wasn't for him.

Travis didn't have much use for the church either, though he was involved in youth ministry as a teenager. By his midtwenties, the church wasn't even on his radar.

Then one day our music team needed a guitar player at the last minute. We offered Travis fifty dollars to play one Sunday morning, and he never left. In the process, he's become one of my closest friends.

What's surprising about Travis is that beneath his ambiguity about the church is a raw, driving passion for the church to actually matter. He gets frustrated with "the show" of Sunday morning worship. Ironically, now as a worship leader, he's concerned that music becomes the focal point of worship more than it should. He'd much rather the church feed homeless people and give them a place to stay than focus first on the quality of the Sunday morning experience.

More than once I've seen Travis personally pick up a panhandler, buy him a meal, and put him in a hotel on his own dime. He cares deeply about the church, but he feels that so much about it is a massive exercise in missing the point. He wants to see the church *live* out its message, not just package the message so people will come to hear it.

Travis is a young adult, and now he's a leader in our church. Sure, I've had to steer him back on course a few times and even hold him accountable when he's dropped a ball or two. But right now, nothing is more important to him than the ministry he's involved in. Travis isn't what you might expect from a young adult if all you read is the stats.

You also might not expect that he has more relationships with older generations than with his own demographic. Travis hangs out regularly with baby boomers (who love him, by the way) and Gen-Xers. He's eager to learn from them. He isn't trying to push older generations out of the way so he can get what he's owed. He's an incredibly hard worker who highly values learning from and being in relationship with older people in his life.

Simply study Travis in a laboratory and you could certainly place many young adult labels on him. But spend time with him and you'll find a picture far more nuanced and profound. You might be surprised and at the same time see something to give you hope for the church's future.

Steering Is Harder Than You Think

Last summer was my first real sailing experience. It didn't take long before I had a major realization: I hate sailing.

A friend who owns a sailboat offered to bring me along on a little expedition. Before that trip, I'll admit my notion of sailing was a bit romantic—some combination of Christopher Columbus and Captain Jack Sparrow.

The reality was more than a little disappointing. Extreme heat, close quarters, and zero attacks by giant squids made this simple out-and-back journey less than the adventure I was hoping for.

I admire that my buddy enjoys such a sophisticated hobby; I really do. But every time I've gone out with him on the boat, I've spent far too much time with my head hanging over the side, losing my lunch.

This time we'd driven from New York City down to Chesapeake Bay with no air conditioning on one of the hottest days of the year. After hours on the road, we were all eager to get the boat out on the water.

The four of us were cramped into a tiny sitting area, knees touching, under the blazing sun. I certainly could have gone below deck if I'd wanted, but it was an Easy-Bake Oven down there. We spent the night on the boat in temperatures so hot all we could do was lie on the deck and try not to melt before falling asleep.

I did learn two useful things on this journey:

✴ I can now unfurl a jib sail anytime I want. I'm basically a pro.

✴ Steering a sailboat is far more difficult than it appears.

Piloting a sailboat, I learned, is quite different from driving a car. In a car, I point the vehicle at the destination, step on the gas, and—barring interruption from traffic lights, pedestrians, large animals, or other vehicles—I'll eventually arrive at my destination.

But sailing isn't simply a matter of setting a target and locking in the cruise control. Sailing requires *constant* adjustments. The wind blows you in one direction but is constantly changing its force. The waves and current move beneath you and pull you, often in a different direction altogether, making steering anything but easy.

Without making continuous adjustments, the boat will miss its target by a mile. Building a young adult ministry requires something similar. With the conditions between you and your destination always changing, you can ill-afford to assume anything and set your ministry on cruise.

This reality is more challenging than we might think. Churches aren't necessarily famous for making adjustments. We're accustomed to setting programs on cruise control and expecting them to get us to our destination. But when the Spirit blows in new directions, doing what comes naturally to us will likely result in drifting farther and farther away from the ministry we've dreamed of.

David Kinnaman of the Barna Group is right when he says:

> The current state of ministry to twentysomethings is woefully inadequate to address the spiritual needs of millions of young adults. These individuals are making significant life choices and determining the patterns and preferences of their spiritual reality while churches wait, generally in vain, for them to return after college or when the kids come.[6]

It's no longer realistic to simply point the ship vaguely in the direction of young adult ministry. We need an elegant, agile solution capable of making constant adjustments based on changing conditions. And one of the first adjustments must be to stop learning *about* young adults and actually build relationships *with* them.

3

Mistake 2

Change the Worship Style

By attempting to attract them with cultural relevance, the church accidentally became irrelevant—like when parents try to be cool. Turns out they don't want their parents to be cool.

JEN HATMAKER, *FOR THE LOVE*

I don't need a friend who changes when I change and who nods when I nod; my shadow does that much better.

PLUTARCH

It was almost midnight in New York City and the clock was about to tick us into the New Year. The temperature outside was a brisk 25 degrees, and crowds of expectant people huddled together for warmth.

I wasn't in Times Square anticipating the famous ball drop. Instead, I was wearing a T-shirt and shorts, shivering in Central Park. I'd flown to the Big Apple to visit a friend, and before I knew it he'd convinced me to enter a four-mile midnight road race.

The clock struck twelve, the gun went off, and I took off running with 4,500 of my newest friends. Bands were playing. Crowds were cheering. Runners even had the option of champagne toasts at each mile marker. It turned out to be quite the celebration!

The most fascinating aspect of the whole experience was the sheer volume of people. There were 4,500 runners, another 5,000 people in the park just for the party, and countless neighbors, friends, and family cheering on the runners at every street corner. It was as if people had nothing better to do on New Year's Eve. At midnight. In New York City.

In a place known for its one-of-a-kind New Year's Eve party in Times Square, I was amazed that this many people would be somewhere else in the city. I wanted to turn to the guy running beside me and ask, "You know there's this really big party going on a few blocks away, right?" That's the thing about New York. It's really good at drawing big crowds!

Churches, on the other hand, tend to have very mixed feelings about crowds.

We know that successful ministry isn't just about numbers. Yet Jesus always seemed to draw big crowds. And most of us sense intuitively that if we're doing something that really connects, more people are likely to show up.

So when we survey the young adult ministry landscape, it's normal that we look for places where young adults are *actually* showing up—places with the biggest crowds. Our natural inclination is to try to imitate what we see those churches doing.

One of the most common strategies for drawing a young adult crowd—and the second-biggest mistake churches make in building a young adult ministry—is to change the church's worship style.

Recently, my coauthor, Mark, had a year away from his role at his church, giving him time for what he hadn't been able to do since starting his ministry—visit loads of other churches. I was fascinated by his observation:

What I learned on my tour of churches is that "contemporary is the new traditional." Even the least likely churches have succumbed to the pressure to do something new and different to attract a younger crowd. I'll never forget walking into the fellowship hall of a delightful church in a suburban neighborhood for their 9:17 (not kidding) "contemporary service." Of the thirty-five or so people there, I'm sure fewer than five of them were under seventy, including the trying-oh-so-hard worship leader, an awkward middle-aged woman holding a microphone complete with an orange pop filter, the out-of-his-element-near-retirement pastor, and a fella with a gray ponytail seated on his amplifier providing wailing, electric guitar solos for almost every song.

Too many churches seem to assume that starting a contemporary worship service holds *the* secret code to bringing back the younger generation. Their biggest mistake is assuming they can (and should) actually pull it off.

It's time for typical traditional churches to face facts. Unless a church is tending to the foundational priorities required to grow a thriving, healthy young adult ministry—what the second half of this book is about—changing the worship style is one more distraction that will accomplish next to nothing.

S.O.W.L. (Save Our Worship Leaders)

Hang around an "ordinary" church long enough these days, and you're likely to hear, "Of course twenty-year-olds aren't coming to our church. Just listen to our music!"

Few topics in a church elicit such strong opinions as music. Everyone has a preference, with many people bolstering their particular musical tastes as somehow more biblical, more theologically orthodox, and less likely to cause someone to stumble. More than a few music ministry jobs have been lost during these decades of debate. And more often, sanity has been sacrificed.

Here's how it happened for Eric. This gifted middle-age musician had been a worship leader in a diverse congregation for twelve years. The church had plenty of grandparents in their sixties, seventies, and eighties—and even more folks in their forties and fifties. In recent years the church had struck a chord with young families in their twenties and thirties. The new senior pastor had a strong vision for reaching teenagers and college students. But leading worship for a congregation that spans seven or eight decades is incredibly challenging.

At a meeting of the strategic planning team, everything hit the fan as leaders read responses from an anonymous church survey:

"The young people hate our music."

"Can we get something written after the Civil War?"

"Every song we sing is so boring."

It seemed pretty clear that the resounding cry of leadership was "more guitar, younger musicians on stage, reach the college students." In equal measure, though, Eric was bombarded by complaints from Sunday worshipers with entirely different opinions:

"Where's the organ?"

"Would it be so hard to sing just *one* hymn?"

"I'm moving to the church down the street, where they still care about people in my generation."

Sadly, more and more worship leaders are caught in a no-win trap. What's even sadder is that changing the worship style, at least as a starting point, almost never moves the needle toward reaching young adults. Here's why.

The Irrelevant Relevance Debate

I need to admit upfront that I lead a hip church that has rock-and-roll worship, electric guitars, and stage lights. It looks awesome. My worship leader is very cool—but not because of skinny jeans or a $200 haircut. He's more like the "I just rolled out of bed and don't know where I am, but I'm going to rock this guitar" kind of cool.

But I'd never tell you to try to replicate our worship style because it "works with young adults." Somebody would get fired.

I lead in a multisite church in the Midwest. Some of our campuses have traditional music. Mine has a more modern selection of worship music. Others have '80s contemporary and still others are "blended," with elements of traditional and contemporary (if we're honest, nobody even knows what those terms mean anymore). And our church has seen young adults come and go within *each* of those settings.

Recently, our hip, young, electric guitar-playing worship leader took a turn leading at our blended worship campus. I watched as some attendees stood silently with their arms crossed, waiting for the noise to be finished, while others passionately engaged in worship.

As I scanned the crowd it was clear there was absolutely no correlation between people's response and their age. After the service, I was fascinated to overhear a conversation between two twenty-somethings who were lifelong friends. They'd grown up together in our community and now had kids the same age. Demographically speaking, they were the same.

One turned to the other and said, "That blew me away. I've been looking for authentic worship like that for a long time. That was amazing!" The other raised his eyebrows and said, "Are you kidding me? I couldn't wait for it to be over!"

It's so easy to make cosmetic changes, thinking that a few external tweaks will help us hit the bull's-eye. We call the sanctuary a "worship center"; we refer to the worship service as an "experience"; we no longer have a "sermon" but "teaching." It's time to be honest and clearly declare that none of these surface changes hold the secret to having young adults actually show up and stay.

Young adults have a long list of reasons they're leaving the church. But the style of worship on Sunday mornings just *isn't* the across-the-board deal breaker it's been assumed to be.

I know I'm committing heresy in some people's minds, but changing your worship style is precisely the wrong place to start.

What Lies Beneath

Rachel Sloan insightfully describes how she views the surface-level approaches most churches take when attempting to attract more young adults:

> The most frustrating part of being a Millennial is that my church does not understand me. Churches often think in this vein: 1) We need more young people in the church. 2) How do we get more young people in the church? 3) We need a room in the church where we can install flashy lights and smoke machines. 4) We need to find a praise band.
>
> If we build it they will come, right? Maybe not.
>
> Despite our love for technology and social media, churches cannot simply slap a contemporary service together, create a Facebook page and call it quits, and then blame us when we do not show up.[1]

Writing for CNN.com, Rachel Held Evans said:

> Time and again, the assumption among Christian leaders, and evangelical leaders in particular, is that the key to drawing 20-somethings back to church is simply to make a few style updates—edgier music, more casual services, a coffee shop in the fellowship hall, a pastor who wears skinny jeans, an up-dated Web site that includes online giving.
>
> What Millennials really want from the church is not a change in style but a change in substance.[2]

In reviewing the young adult response to Evans's article, Brett McCracken, author of *Hipster Christianity: When Church and Cool Collide*, points out that, "The line that I saw shared on Facebook more than any other is this, 'We're not leaving the church because we don't find the cool factor there; we're leaving the church because we don't find Jesus there.'"[3]

Could it be that, despite the popular caricature, young adults *don't* want to be catered to?

Hopefully by now you're starting to hear the steady drumbeat: young adults aren't looking to your church to create the coolest new program where they can attend as spectators.

Read that last sentence again*: young adults aren't looking to your church to create the coolest new program where they can attend as spectators.*

I know, you're not convinced. You're thinking: If young adults don't want to be catered to and if changing the worship style isn't the key ingredient, then why are young adults in our town flocking to the one hip church that *does* cater to them?

And you'd be right.

Almost every major city now has at least one large (often multi-site) church that puts on a worship production every Sunday specifically targeting young adults. And in many of those places, young adults are leaving the churches they grew up in and showing up in droves to the cool new production.

How then can I possibly say with a straight face that young adults aren't looking to be spectators of great programs, geared especially to their tastes?

Consistent with their paradoxical nature, both realities are true for young adults.

* They long for something beyond a consumer role in the church.

As one commentator writes, "They are looking for true, deep, intellectually robust spirituality in their parents' churches and not finding it."[4]

* At the same time, their attendance patterns indicate that, at least on one level, they absolutely *are* looking for a place where they can be consumers of excellent music and compelling, entertaining teaching.

I'm not arguing that new churches (they're almost *always* new) with a worship focus on young adults don't work, but that *when a traditional church tries to imitate the worship of the hip church in town, it almost never works.*

When an established church (with very little budget or stomach for production) decides that "for the sake of reaching the next generation" it will create an "alternative worship service," it almost always turns out to be an embarrassingly poor imitation of cool. Awkward musicians, usually in their fifties, step out of choir robes for an hour to hold microphones and sway uncomfortably as they sing Chris Tomlin songs. They call it contemporary, but it's usually closer to hip replacement than to hip.

Changing your worship style to attract young adults almost never works for a few very good reasons:

1. Young adults aren't all of one mind in their worship-style tastes.

2. Very few churches have the resources to pull off excellent, compelling, contemporary worship week after week.

3. There's a massive difference between a new church that launches with the DNA of newer styles of worship and an established church that tries to affix a newer worship service onto the side of its core ministry.

4. A poorly executed contemporary service is more of a young adult repellent than a high-quality, highbrow traditional service ever could be.

I may be dreaming here, but I'd like to declare the traditional-contemporary worship-style debate over. Continuing this conversation, especially when it comes to building a young adult ministry where none exists, is a massive exercise in missing the point. Changing our worship style (or any other modernizing change, for that matter) isn't a bad thing. Most churches certainly could use a little more innovation when it comes to worship!

Your church may need to change its worship style; just don't do it as a starting strategy for reaching the next generation. When it comes to building a sustainable young adult ministry, updating to a "young adult friendly" worship style should be more like step three hundred, rather than step one, in a five hundred-step process.

The great news is that if your church can't afford (because of financial reasons, church politics, or lack of volunteers) to create a high-production, attractive worship experience for young adults, you still can create a thriving young adult ministry.

The Slow Road to Success

Big, sweeping changes to worship can be a costly venture for a congregation. It costs leadership credibility, time, and energy—and often can cost members.

Though it's usually painful and risky, changing your church's worship style is a *surface-level* solution to a much more complex challenge. The solution starts with the awareness that *no* external change can provide a quick fix.

While most churches focus on quick changes they can make in order to get young adults in the door, few have thought through a clear vision and game plan to integrate them into the leadership and fundamental DNA of the church.

Let's take a few years for a moratorium on the quick-fix worship overhauls in the name of reaching young adults. Let's focus instead on building a ministry to young adults that's effective in the long haul.

Mistake 3

Expect the Youth Director to Do It

> *Cheap saddles ain't good, and good saddles ain't cheap.*
>
> COWBOY PROVERB

> *If you think it's expensive to hire a professional
> to do the job, wait until you hire an amateur.*
>
> RED ADAIR

I'm a sucker for reality TV, so much so that my wife and I were actually featured on a reality show where viewers watched us buy a house. (Spoiler alert: we went for the third house.) Who knew something as mundane as house hunting could create television that millions of people *choose* to watch every week?

My favorite reality show is *Extreme Cheapskates*, which takes saving money to ridiculous extremes. Viewers watch families ration their food and toilet paper, mixing one part juice to five parts water.

One mom went so far as to count Cheerios for her toddler son: "We're going to give you fourteen," she said as she counted. As he gobbled up the meager pile, she gently reminded him, "And remember, you need to eat all your Cheerios or next time you only get twelve."[1]

Although going to such lengths to save a buck or two might feel responsible, sometimes the least expensive approach winds up costing much more in the long run.

That feels a lot like what most churches try to do with their young adult ministries. We need it, but we want it quick and cheap. If it worked, we'd all sing the Doxology, churches would be financially responsible, and there'd be no need for this book. But our national track record of abysmal young adult ministry suggests that the quick and cheap approach never gets us what we're looking for.

One of the most common patterns we see in young adult ministry is for church leadership to walk down the hall, find the youth director's office, and add a new title to the nameplate: Director of Youth *and* Young Adults.

It seems so logical, doesn't it?

After all, most youth directors are still young adults themselves, often making them the one person in the church who actually *knows* young adults. It seems so economical; it won't cost the church any more money and won't increase the staff head count. And it feels like such a natural fit. A youth director who's been around a few years knows the college students and young adults who've been part of the youth ministry.

It makes so much sense—and is also a huge mistake.

The Grand Mismatch

A local youth worker named Jesse called me to have coffee. His church had decided it was time to do *something* to reach young adults. Leaders asked Jesse to start a ministry to young adults. "It won't take that much time," the personnel committee chair said. "Just a Bible study once a week or something like that. We think you're the guy for the job!" Being a young adult in his first full-time job, Jesse was eager to prove himself and impress the committee.

Jesse began asking me question after question. It didn't take long to realize he's an incredibly talented guy with lots of potential. In youth ministry now for five years, Jesse plays guitar in his own band. His marriage is about a year old and he has plenty of relationships with other young people like him. He has the kinds of qualifications almost any church would look for in a person to head up the mission of reaching young adults.

I had a hunch, though, from that first meeting, that this arrangement was set up for failure. And sure enough, Jesse spent only a single semester with "and Young Adults" attached to his "Director of Youth" title. Even worse, the church gave up trying to do young adult ministry altogether after this attempt failed to produce any sustainable results.

It wasn't because Jesse was a bad guy. It wasn't because he didn't have the skills, and it wasn't because he didn't care. It was because his church's approach was fundamentally flawed from the beginning.

There are three basic reasons:

1. This approach seldom allots the necessary and unique leadership resources needed to create a sustainable young adult ministry.

2. This approach assumes that success in young adult ministry should come naturally, without much effort, when national trends show exactly the opposite.

3. This approach sets the stage for young adults to be isolated from church life.

Lack of Time

Try this homework assignment: find a few youth workers in your church or community and ask how much time they spend in any given week wondering what to do with their spare time. I doubt you'll find any with such a problem on their hands.

Most youth workers I know are stretched and stressed. Assigning the youth worker to oversee a young adult ministry without adding any hours to their weekly schedule is choosing *cheap*—not just inexpensive but cheap. It's a choice to overload the youth worker in a way that can't help but negatively impact their own work—with youth, young adults, or both. It's a choice to underresource and undervalue young adult ministry from the outset. It's a choice that says, "It would be nice if this worked, but we don't really care to invest in its success."

Making young adults another side plate for a youth director to spin is a rapid route to ensure high frustration and little reward. And because young adults are the largest generation in American history, it also reveals we're not taking the challenge seriously.

Though we may assume there are similarities, working with eighteen- to thirty-year-olds is actually staggeringly different from working with twelve- to eighteen-year-olds. Unless it was part of their original contract, most youth workers didn't sign on to lead a young adult ministry. Tacking it onto the end of a job description is a huge bait-and-switch proposition for the youth worker and the church, requiring additional tools, resources, and skill sets.

Insufficient Focus

Young adult ministry is tough. A tiny fraction of churches are, by their own estimation, succeeding with young adults. Unlike the field of youth ministry that has, over the past twenty years or so, developed clear norms, best practices, and training systems, young adult ministry is pioneer work. The tracks haven't been laid. No well-worn path takes young adult leaders to their destination.

Most are clearly lost.

Think about it this way. Would you ask a sixteen-year-old to start your youth ministry? Would you ask a second-grader to start your children's ministry? They might have great hearts and a real desire to succeed—and lots of relationships among the target population— but their chances of success are infinitesimal.

Most churches expect to create a thriving young adult ministry by throwing at it a few extra, misdirected, uninformed hours. The results are predictable: programs that start and sputter, launch and fizzle, and never quite get off the ground.

Structured Isolation

Ministry to young adults is wholly different from youth ministry. Yet so many churches end up building a young adult ministry that looks eerily similar to their youth ministry—Sunday morning class, fellowship activities, small groups, retreats, and a few service projects.

Despite the popular language that "youth aren't the church of tomorrow; they're the church of today," a key component of any youth ministry is still *preparing* teenagers for lifelong Christian adulthood. Placing this same lens over young adult ministry is highly problematic.

With this lens, churches end up creating an alternative universe for young adults, one that keeps them in a subadult category with few, if any, on-ramps to integration and leadership in the church. The natural result is young adults who are isolated from the rest of the church body, cordoned off until they marry, have children, establish careers, and are ready to become "real" contributing members of the church. When we keep young adults in this kind of holding pattern, it's completely understandable why so few actually stick around.

All three of these reasons—lack of time, insufficient focus, and structured isolation—point to a fundamental flaw in this approach: a lack of appropriate investment. It's tough to succeed in any enterprise when we treat it as an afterthought.

Like trying to stay warm under a 4' x 4' blanket, underresourced ministries chronically struggle to maintain success for very long. Few if any churches ever build a thriving young adult ministry by treating it as a sidebar to, or an extension of, the youth ministry. Instead, this approach essentially ensures that the church continues defining success with young adults inaccurately.

Success becomes defined as the youth pastor corralling young adults in programs, doing whatever it takes to keep them coming. Instead of leveraging this generation's passion and power to bring their voice to the table and bring vitality to the church, we box young adults into a holding pattern with little thought of actually treating them as young *adults.*

Success Reconsidered

The room held an impressive, intimidating air about it. In the center was a large mahogany table heavy enough to bear the weight of huge decisions. Sixteen large leather chairs surrounded the table. Floor-to-ceiling windows gave the room a sense of brightness, hope, and positive energy.

Ryan was interviewing for a position as the director of high school ministry at a large church. Not only were all sixteen seats filled, but also a few more had been brought in to accommodate additional interviewers.

Parents, staff members, volunteers, as well as all the senior-level pastors had gathered to invest in what they all felt was a game-changing decision for the church—hiring the *right* high school director. Clearly, this was more of a big-league interview than Ryan anticipated.

I definitely felt the anxiety, for both him and myself. If hired, Ryan would be working for me in the youth ministry I was charged to oversee.

Our high school ministry had struggled in recent months, which produced a significant dip in attendance. Enthusiasm and goodwill were in short supply. Students were bored. Parents were panicky and anxious. A lot was riding on this interview because the church desperately wanted a win.

In the end, Ryan was invited to ask questions. "Tell me about success," he said. "What does success look like for this position?"

One pastor spoke up without missing a beat: "Around three hundred to four hundred in attendance for weekly programs and at least a thousand for outreach events."

I remember little else about the interview. My inner monologue took over: *Four hundred kids at a weekly program? We're getting only sixty now! A thousand high school students? Are there even that many in our whole town?*

The numbers floored me, not because they were big but because of how *success* was being defined. My pastor's response (which was brand-new information to me, by the way) reminded me how fuzzy and confusing it can be to define *success* in any ministry.

Large numbers of attendees are the most obvious mark of success. If people are coming, we must be doing something right, right? Excitement and enthusiasm can be markers of success; if we *feel* great about the ministry, it must *be* great, right? Stories of life change can be measures of success because "if we change just one person's life . . ."

And you could argue that youth ministry throughout America is succeeding by all these measures.

Youth pastors can tell stories of deep-impact life change in their students. More youth may be attending our programs and events than ever before. More resources and value are being assigned to this segment of the church's ministry than ever before. And we have more formally educated, professional youth pastors (equipped with actual degrees in youth ministry) than ever before.

We could reasonably argue that youth ministry as a whole has never been more "successful" than it is right now, based on all the traditional markers of success. That's all the more reason to give these successful youth directors charge over ministry to young adults, right?

Unfortunately, that's almost always the exact wrong choice.

Unsticky Faith

The Fuller Youth Institute at Fuller Seminary recently completed six years of "Sticky Faith" research through its College Transition Project. For many people involved in youth ministry, this is the first real look at what happens to students *after* they leave the programs. The results are less than encouraging.

Of students who were actively engaged in youth programs when they graduated from high school, research shows that only about 40 to 50 percent actually stick with their faith through college.[2] If the trend holds true, in an average youth group, one out of every two high school seniors who are currently *active* in our ministries will shed their involvement in the church as they shed their caps and gowns.

These are the *insider* kids—not the "once in a blue moon" kids or the "I see them at school events" kids. Half of the most active youth group kids are disconnecting from the church and their faith by the time they graduate from college! In an age when the machine of youth ministry is running as high-octane as ever, graduates are making a mass exodus from faith.

Barna Group research is even more discouraging: "The most potent data regarding disengagement is that a majority of twenty-somethings—61 percent of today's young adults—had been churched at one time during their teen years but they are now spiritually disengaged (i.e., not actively attending church, reading the Bible, or praying)."[3]

Stated another way, the long-term effectiveness of "successful" youth ministry (e.g., ones that keep young people coming to programs targeted specifically to them) is being called into question more and more these days. We must ask: Does it make sense to apply this shortsighted definition of *success* to ministry with young adults and college students?

Two Thousand Dollar Shoes

I'd finally achieved a big goal I'd been working toward for a long time. I crossed the finish line of my very first 25K race. I ran (okay, *mostly* ran) 15.5 miles on a rainy morning in May and subsequently thought two things:

1. I can't believe how good I feel to have completed this race.

2. I can't believe how awful I feel right now.

Eight months of daily training went into this race. At first, the going was pretty easy, a mile or two on every run. The leaves were changing color, I felt good, and everything was great. But then the two-mile runs turned into five, six, and beyond. Before I knew it, I was setting my alarm to run for an hour in the dark each morning. Some days I'd run eight miles in ten-degree weather. But now, I'd finally crossed the finish line.

However, in this case, the finish line was just the beginning.

The day after the race, something popped in the top of my foot while I was standing at church. I immediately started limping, trying to avoid the significant pain that came with every step.

I had no idea what I was dealing with.

After two weeks of rest, I started running again, only a mile at a time. And the pain returned every time I increased my mileage. So I'd rest for a couple more weeks, and the cycle would repeat itself.

I finally went to a physical therapist, who spent the next three months (and the next thousand dollars of my health insurance deductible) on exercises and painful deep-tissue massage. He recommended I replace my old orthotics with a fifty dollar pair of over-the-counter ones and finally discharged me when the pain was better, though not quite gone.

Still, the more I ran, the more the pain returned. So I went to the doctor, who took an x-ray, then an MRI, and sent me to an orthopedic specialist. She recommended a new set of orthotics and a couple of (painful) cortisone shots in the top of my foot.

I sat down with the custom orthotic specialist and retold the story of the past nine months. The more I talked, the more depressed I became. I had other races in mind—races I'd paid for and had to scrap because of my foot pain. I had other things I wanted to do with that thousand dollars I'd spent on physical therapy and the almost five hundred dollars on other copays. And I certainly wasn't thrilled about the additional four hundred dollars I was about to spend on custom orthotics.

But at least I was finally getting some results. The shot had taken effect, and the support from the new orthotics seemed to be the fix. Finally, after all this time, money, and anxiety, I was about to start making progress again.

Before long, the specialist looked at my shoes and asked, "Are those the shoes you run in?"

I nodded, and he said, "I'm not sure what you paid for those. They may be fine. But as a general rule, I tell my running patients that paying more for your shoes is the smartest thing you can do. You should spend at least ninety to one hundred dollars for your shoes because they'll give you the right kind of support, especially if you run long distances. With running shoes, you get what you pay for. Fifty-dollar shoes can lead to serious problems."

I stopped in my tracks, immediately recalling a conversation with a coworker from the previous fall as I was beginning my training. We were comparing shoes, and he said, "I don't know, man, that seems like a terrible decision."

"No way!" I responded. "Why would I spend a hundred dollars on shoes at a running store when these cost me fifty-five bucks at Walmart? I love them!"

I didn't give that conversation a second thought until that moment in the clinic silently calculating how much that fifty-five dollar pair of shoes had actually cost me. My decision to save forty-five bucks ended up costing close to two thousand, not to mention lost time, depression, anxiety, and pain. It was a huge price to pay for saving forty-five bucks.

I worry that many churches are making extremely expensive choices—to save money and energy—that turn out to be just as costly, if not more so, to the next generation.

I'm not saying a full-time staff person is required for a successful young adult ministry. But starting a young adult ministry with a bargain-priced arrangement of adding a few hours onto the youth worker (who won't likely get paid any more for the additional effort and time) almost never works. This is a classic case of a money-saving strategy that doesn't actually save money. Sometimes what looks like a good deal ends up hurting more than it helps.

Dropping additional responsibilities onto a youth director's plate is a knee-jerk solution that seldom provides enough horsepower to meet the challenge of ministry with young adults. It's the wrong model, and it almost never works.

So before you tack that "and Young Adults" onto the youth director's job title, consider what kind of investment you're making in your young adult ministry. Consider the ramifications for your youth ministry. Consider the cost of not fully engaging the mission to young adults that your church might desperately need. In the end, this "money-saving" approach can turn out to be more expensive than building it right in the first place.

Mistake 4

Start by Creating a Young Adult Program

> *The church had decided they wanted a college program
> to reach out to students in the area. The congregation wanted
> a college program. The elders wanted a college program.
> The staff wanted a college program. But in the end it was
> a lot of rhetoric, and no one really wanted to invest
> in a long-term strategy. When we restructured our ministry
> eighteen months later, they eliminated my position.
> No one really thought about [young adult ministry]
> as a real investment that needed a five-year plan.*
>
> FORMER YOUNG ADULT PASTOR

> *People who are good with a hammer treat
> everything like a nail.*
>
> AMERICAN PROVERB

My wife is on a new kick. She wants to go on a family vacation to the Grand Canyon. When she says "family vacation," she's talking about an old-fashioned road trip in our minivan. Actually, she'd like it better if it were a '72 station wagon with wood paneling and no air conditioning.

But I digress.

We live in Michigan, so we're talking three days on the road—each way. Apparently, my wife believes long hours of monotony in a cramped space with young children somehow equals "vacation." She says getting there is half the fun, and the journey is more important than the destination. You get the idea.

When I mention all the things about this trip that could be potentially miserable, my wife doesn't see problems. She actually gets excited about what she calls the "hard parts." She wants to prohibit us from taking the quick route. That's right: she prefers the long, endless journey and endless games of I Spy. She may find the idea nostalgic, but I find it torturous. Thanks, but no thanks.

My plan would be to get on a plane, arrive in a few hours, stand atop the canyon, snap some pictures, make sure our kids notice there's a big hole in the ground, and then hit the hotel pool for the rest of the trip. Now *that's* vacation!

In my saner moments, I know my wife is right. She wants our kids to have a shared experience with us. For my wife, seeing the Grand Canyon is fine, but the trip itself is what holds the promise of shaping our family.

Unfortunately, when it comes to ministry with young adults, most churches choose my vacation approach. They want to get to the destination as quickly as possible. They want to set up a program or two for young adults to flock to. Most churches that start a young adult ministry don't even consider the slow route of developing a *strategic* plan of any kind. They'd rather push the easy button labeled "program."

What's Wrong With Programs?

Almost every church follows a similar startup cycle for young adult ministry that looks like this:

Step 1. Buy some pizza and invite college students or twenty-somethings to stay after a worship service to discuss how to reach their friends. Print an announcement in the bulletin to get young adults there.

Step 2. Launch some version of a college and career group designed to reach young adults. In addition, add a combination of get-to-know-you games, volleyball, and, of course, more pizza.

Step 3. Watch in utter amazement six months (or six weeks) later as the ministry fizzles out and the disappointed two or three active young adults wonder what's wrong with them.

Step 4. Blame the megachurches and their seeker-sensitive approach. Blame competition from parachurch ministries. Blame the consumerist young adults.

Step 5. Repeat the same exact process in a few years or as soon as the church has forgotten the last attempt (whichever comes first).

Why, you may wonder, do churches keep going back to the same well, where there's clearly no water? Because they assume providing better programs is the right answer to every problem.

For children, it was changing from boring Sunday school to Promiseland or Name-of-your-church Kidz. For teenagers, the church upgraded from young people's societies and youth groups to events with youth bands and cool names such as Blaze, Ignite, and Fuel. (Is it just me, or has anyone else noticed how many youth groups choose names related to burning things?) When we had trouble getting teenagers in the door, we created events such as Pizza Olympics and Crud Wars.

And it worked.

Sort of.

At least our well-marketed and well-designed programming kept a critical mass of young people coming, even if the vast majority of older youth dropped out of weekly programming in their last years of high school. Our first approach to reaching young adults is often to create new programs because it's what churches know how to do.

Pastor Matthew Marino questions whether this approach really was a success after all:

> It was the drug everyone wanted: Parents wanted their kids to like church. Pastors wanted undistracted parents listening to their sermons. Worship leaders wanted to avoid the complexity of pleasing multiple generations. Youth pastors liked the numbers and accolades. Kids liked the band and shorter message. On top of that, donors were excited to write large checks to build expensive facilities with the promise of reaching lost and hurting kids. And if our metrics are seats filled and satisfaction surveys, it looked like it was working. *But what are the long-term effects of segregated, program-driven ministry?*[1]

The long-term effects of this approach are staring us in the face as we look at the next generation. Why would the approach that couldn't keep them around be the very same approach we take to get them back?

Young adults have "been there, done that" and got the T-shirt. And it's not what they're looking for.

The Wrong Question

The primary question churches seem to be asking young adults is, "What kind of *program* do you want the church to provide for you?" I think it's time to ask a different question.

Young adults such as Rachel Sloan may help us get closer to the right question. She says,

> We want churches that want to have a relationship with us.
>
> We do not want churches to immediately advertise to us how great their contemporary service is, how amazing their

young adult Sunday school class is, how sizable their group of young adults is, as if to say: "Of course we want you here! Just stay in your niche where we cannot see you and have fun over there while the rest of us run the church and make the big decisions."

We do not want you to immediately shove us off to a part of the church where we will never be seen or heard from again. . . . Whatever your church does well, there is a faction of Millennials that wants to be a part of it. Is your church passionate about social justice, worship, or ministry to the local community? Do that, focus on that, and Millennials may end up at your church.

Then let us help you do that. We do not only want to attend church on Sunday morning. Many of us care and want to be involved in a church; we just have not found ones that will let us in.

We are not going to a church that does not care about our ideas, and we are not going to a church that is not willing to fully embrace us. Would you?[2]

If not a young adult *program,* then what *are* they looking for? Author Jen Hatmaker points out what the latest research reveals:

When young adults between ages eighteen and thirty-five were polled nationwide and asked, "What would draw you or keep you at a church?" they listed the following four tenets:
1. Community
2. Social justice
3. Depth
4. Mentorship[3]

In short, young adults are looking for ways to connect and for opportunities to change the world with the gospel. They're looking for roles integral to the mission of our churches. They're looking for a place where they can make a difference. They're looking for a seat at the table and for people and organizations to partner with in making an impact in their community.

What they don't need (and, mostly, don't want) is to be compartmentalized into an insular group that participates in, with nauseating familiarity, a polished-up version of youth group.

Young adults aren't just looking to be attracted to your church; they're looking to be connected to it. They're looking for more than the hidden message beneath most young adult programming: "Warm bodies welcome."

Programs specific to young adults typically provide young adults little opportunity to be woven into the fabric of your church or integrated into a church's life and leadership. Age-specific programs do little to affirm people's contributions to the church as a whole. The sad truth we're afraid to face is that most age-specific young adult programming doesn't even *temporarily* attract young adults, let alone engage the depth of relationship or mentorship they seek. It leaves most of them disinterested, disconnected, and undervalued.

If a young adult program is your starting point for connecting with young adults, you've missed the heart of what they actually seek from the church. Although your goal of reaching this generation is right on target, the strategy of *starting* with a young adult program shoots you in the foot from day one.

They Want to Change the World

I recently ran into a twenty-three-year-old friend named Thomas, who grew up in the same town I did. He was raised by upper-middle-class parents, enjoyed a Christian K-12 education, and was deeply involved in his local church.

Thomas was the classic church kid and a typical high school student. No great tragedies. No great triumphs. He was well-liked.

He argued with his parents. He stayed out of trouble. He planned to attend a local private college after high school.

But a few years into that experience, Thomas decided to leave college and go to film school. He had found his voice as an artist and discovered a love for filmmaking. Thomas created his own film company to express his art and tell stories. But more than making good movies, Thomas wants to change the world—not by making more "Christian" movies but by being a Christian making movies.

During lunch, Thomas told me, "I'm at this point in my life where I'm excited about the film company I run and the projects I get to work on, but I really want to figure out how my business can make a real impact in this world for good."

Thomas isn't alone among young adults.

In a 2011 study on social change, Walden University reported that in the last year, 81 percent of young adults had "donated money, goods, or services as a way to actively take part in the betterment of their world."[4] An overwhelming majority of young adults profoundly embrace their role as change agents in the world.

Young adults such as Thomas long for the church to come alongside them and provide a platform for putting their faith into action in world-changing ways. They don't want more games. They don't want to sit in another chair in front of another stage. And they don't need more pizza.

The church has a choice: we can work to figure out how to activate the eighty million young adults for the sake of the gospel, or we can watch from the sidelines as they change the world without the church.

Gabe Lyons, author and founder of Q Ideas, a learning community that mobilizes Christians to advance the common good in society, describes the subtle shift in emphasis in how young adults (what he calls "the Next Christians") see salvation: "The Next Christians believe that Christ's death and resurrection were not only meant to save people FROM something. He wanted to save Christians TO something."[5]

A first focus on "get them to show up to something they'll like" programs is a fundamentally flawed approach. Sure, like every age group, young adults can be motivated by a big crowd. But their deep longings (and the focus most likely to keep them engaged) are connection, impact, and making change.

If you're wondering how in the world your church can pull off something as nebulous as helping young adults make an impact, hang with me. In the second half of this book, I'll set out a deliberate process to help you accomplish that very thing.

Putting Programming in Its Place

Let me be clear, lest you miss what I'm trying to say: a young adult or college program isn't wrong, but as the starting place for young adult ministry, it is painfully problematic.

True to their paradoxical nature, young adults value relationships with older generations and are looking for intergenerational relationships, but they typically aren't texting baby boomer friends on Friday nights to hang out. They're *also* looking (sometimes desperately) for a place to enjoy and build healthy friendships with their peers.

Providing space (and, yes, programming) in your church for college students and young adults to find and connect to each other will be essential, eventually. Young adult programs aren't without value; they're simply not the place to begin.

Young adults send mixed signals to older generations about what they really want and need for a good reason: they need both. For them, it's not an either-or choice between a place to be connected to an intergenerational community or a place to be with peers. It's a both-and experience.

Later I'll explain why starting with intergenerational relationship systems almost always results in expanded peer relationships and why a steady diet of peer-based programming alone typically results in neither.

Although life-stage programs may scratch the itch *we* have for a quick fix and offer us a comfortable starting point for young adult ministry, in the long run this approach almost always fails to give them (and us) what we're looking for.

Mistake 5

Wait Until They're Ready

The world is all gates, all opportunities,
strings of tension waiting to be struck.

RALPH WALDO EMERSON

"Are you ready?" Klaus asked finally.
"No," Sunny answered.
"Me neither," Violet said, "but if we wait until we're ready
we'll be waiting for the rest of our lives. Let's go."

LEMONY SNICKET, *THE ERSATZ ELEVATOR*

My family recently moved to the southern edge of our community's development. My home is part of a brand-new subdivision, and our lot is right on the dividing line between suburbia and acres of rural farmland.

Just out my back door, I see barns full of tractors, silos filled with grain, and fields bursting with crops as they meet the horizon. Last week I pulled our car to the side of the road so my kids and I could see a hay baler in action. We watched, mesmerized, as the tractor drove back and forth across the field, launching fresh hay bales into its trailer, one by one, for almost an hour.

Maybe this newfound fascination caused my ear to tune in when NPR recently reported about the future of farming.

> Bob Hawthorn is standing in the back of a red pickup in an open field, on a windy April afternoon in Iowa's Loess Hills. This is where he farms 2,000 acres of corn and soybeans, and he's eager to get his crop into the ground. Hawthorn is 84 years old. His hands are worn from all those years of hard work. And he gets annoyed when his neighbors ask just how long he plans to continue that. . . .
>
> In the meantime, for those coveting the land, it could be a long wait. In Iowa, nearly a third of farmland belongs to people over 75. That means farmers like Bob Hawthorn hold a big piece of the future of farming.

Agricultural economist Mike Duffy says a new generation is ready to work the land but may have a hard time getting hold of it: "We aren't short of young people that want to farm. We're short of old people who want to move over."[1]

That line struck a chord with me because the same thing could be said about most churches.

As pastor's kids, my young boys are also fascinated with church right now. They love everything about Jesus, Sunday school, and singing worship songs. And in ten years or so, when they enter the world of adulthood, will the church hold them back and keep them waiting in the wings? Or will the church find a way to share leadership? Based on our current trajectory, I'm nervous.

Most churches today simply keep the young adults they *do* have in a holding pattern—often unintentionally. They push the pause button and say, "We'll get back to you when you're *ready*." Although this mistake may be unintentional, it's as widespread and damaging as the others.

I'm not suggesting that older generations simply get out of the way in a mass exodus of leadership. We don't need an abrupt hand-off from older, experienced leaders to totally green ones. That would be a disaster.

Here's what I'm affirming:

1. Apprenticeship is absolutely essential for young church leaders.

2. The typical church is doing next to nothing to actually apprentice young adults into meaningful leadership roles.

In today's church, "apprenticeship" easily can be church-speak for "wait just a little longer."

The Long Wait

Young adults today have grown up in an increasingly accessible world. Here are some results of a recent survey of parents by a computer-security software company:

* Sixty-six percent of kids ages three, four, and five can play a computer game, but only 58 percent can ride a bike.

* Thirty-eight percent of those children can write their full names and 14 percent can tie their shoes (a skill that's usually mastered by age six), compared to 57 percent who know how to operate a tablet.

* Forty-seven percent of young children can operate a smartphone, while parents report that only 26 percent know how to make their own breakfast.[2]

For their entire lives, young adults have literally had the world at their fingertips. As kids they're interconnected with the world around them, and today they've grown into CEOs of tech startups, small-business owners, and founders of nonprofits by the time they're in their midtwenties.

Many popular sports figures and cultural icons are downright ancient by the time they hit thirty-five. Yet this is the generation most churches sideline for leadership because they're not "ready." Australian ministry specialist Fuzz Kitto remarks.

> I have a friend who, when he was 23, had an income of over $100,000 a year. He managed over 1,000 employees. Decisions he made before breakfast affected the economic policies of the entire Australian region. "But when I go to church," he reflected, "they treat me like a kid."
>
> In another congregation in which I served as a consultant, a 25 year old who was a consultant accountant managing a multimillion dollar budget was rejected as a member of the finance committee. The reason: "He's too young and inexperienced to understand how the finances of the church really work, and as a single person he hasn't had to deal with the major life issues of balancing a budget for his family." In other words, "He's not an adult."[3]

I recently read about a church that was in the process of electing the next group of elders to the board. As they discussed potential nominees for the position, they spent lots of time talking about a particular thirty-five-year-old nominee. They decided that although he had spiritual and leadership qualifications, he was "just too young" to hold such a leadership position as an elder in their church. Instead, they elected him an "elder-in-training."

Isn't it fascinating that someone old enough to be elected president of the United States often isn't considered old enough to hold a significant leadership position in many of our churches?

Young adults are fast becoming our culture's leading innovators, business leaders, entertainment icons, and world changers. And what is the church telling them? *You're not quite ready yet. Maybe after you've paid your dues and been a faithful attender and contributor for a few more decades, we'll invite you to serve on a committee.*

This reality is, of course, less about young adults being ready and more about our lack of a clear process to move them into leadership. It's probably also about the rest of us trying to hold onto the wheel just a little bit longer.

Author and pastor Larry Osborne puts it this way: "Leadership is a zero-sum game. One person's emerging influence is always another person's waning influence. That's why making room for the young eagles is a hard sell, especially to those who already have a place at the table."[4]

Is it any surprise that this mistake leaves young adults more than a little disinterested in the church?

Meet Andrew

I had lunch with Andrew this week while he was home from college. I knew him as a high school student when I was a youth pastor. There's something magnetic about Andrew. Everyone seems to love him. When he was young, he was teased for smiling all the time. And he might be the smartest person I've ever met.

Andrew recently finished six months of teaching little kids in Ghana. When he returns to school next semester, he wants to start a church in a lecture hall on campus, focusing particularly on students in sororities and fraternities who might never darken a church door.

When people ask Andrew about his plans to attend seminary and begin preparations to be a pastor, his reply is a simple, "No thanks." Andrew doesn't want to prepare to *become* a pastor. He sees himself as a pastor right now.

There is, of course, a danger in this kind of impatience. Doctors don't simply start practicing medicine without appropriate training.

But still, Andrew's response reveals something about the essential shift in perspective churches must make with a generation that wants to offer something of significance to the world *now*.

Failing the Development Test

Apart from going to seminary and becoming a pastor, the on ramps to real leadership in the church for young adults are few and far between. Despite the fact that almost every church laments it doesn't have enough volunteers to fill all the needed roles, most key leadership positions are already filled with an old guard who's resistant to step aside. (And they characteristically complain that all the work falls to a small group of "committed" leaders in the church.)

In his book *Sticky Teams*, Osborne suggests: "The seniors never graduate (at least not until they've become literal seniors and start dying off). They hog the leadership table, shutting out the next generation. It's one of the main reasons that most churches stop growing and lose their evangelistic touch (and cultural relevance) around the twenty-year mark."[5]

Ironically, the same churches that complain the loudest about the lack of young volunteers often have absolutely zero developmental process for them. They bemoan young adults' lack of commitment. They blame young adults for not knowing the way to get things done in the church, but the typical church isn't helping them get there.

Despite what most churches *say* they want, only a tiny fraction of churches have taken the time to design and implement a process for recruiting, building, and developing young leaders. As a result, young adults hear a mind-numbing refrain: "These aren't the leadership roles you're looking for. Move along. Move along" (cue *Star Wars* music).

And they do move along—right out of the church.

Let's admit the layered mistakes most churches are making.

* First, we have no way of assessing a young adult's readiness to lead.

* Second, we have no process for helping young people grow toward mature spiritual leadership.

* Third, we have few meaningful leadership roles to place them in once they *are* prepared.

No wonder so many Christian young adults believe they have a better chance of making an impact for the gospel by working at Toms Shoes than in the church.

First Steps

Our church recently made a first attempt at remedying this problem. We initiated a leadership-development course especially for young adults. We articulated the outcomes, developed a pathway for them to follow, and recruited a group to pilot the process.

As I sat at the table for the first session, I listened to each person describe their calling. For some, it was the beginning of a road to full-time ministry, but most were everyday young adults eager for a shot at church leadership. As one young woman put it, "God's been calling me as a leader for a long time, and I want to find a way to live that out."

I began to wonder, *What would've happened if we had failed to create this process? Where would those callings have been addressed?*

In another church? Maybe.

At the end of their lives as mere unrealized potential?

Would they one day doubt they had actually experienced God's call at all?

Who's listening to our young adults who hear the whispers of God's call to leadership? Can churches create pathways for young adults that actually prepare them for faithful leadership?

Reality Check

When we hear comments like, "A family in our church was asked to host a dinner for twenty-somethings. Twelve RSVP'd yes. No one showed up," the Gen-Xers and boomers in the room nod with passionate disapproval.

There's another (quite reasonable) reason churches sideline young leaders. Young adults can be notoriously unreliable, *even* when they're passionate about something.

Those of us who have young adult friends know it's true. Some of my closest friends are fifty-fifty on showing up for a social event, even when they tell me they'll be there.

One writer and political activist describes organizing a phone bank to encourage the community to act on a cause she knew was near and dear to the hearts of her young adult friends. She sent a day-of reminder to young adults who'd already said they'd be there, and here's a sampling of what she heard back:

* "Oh no, something came up."
* "I don't think I'll be able to. I'm really busy."
* "I *totally* forgot about a family thing tonight, sorry."[6]

The pendulum-swing unpredictability about young adult leadership can be unnerving. In the 2008 US presidential election, the record-high turnout of eighteen- to twenty-nine-year-olds played a huge role in the result. Yet just two years later, the young adult vote dropped by 60 percent.

Most twenty-somethings score consistently higher on the *dreams* meter than on the *follow-through* meter.

* It's part opportunity. Vast interconnectedness has given them more choices than they can prioritize.
* It's part youthfulness. Let's be honest, you and I weren't great decision-makers at twenty-two either.
* But it's also partly our own fault.

We have the opportunity to *cultivate* reliability and leadership among young adults. Instead, most churches bounce erratically between expecting perfection and expecting nothing at all.

What would happen if we changed our expectations? What if we focused on *developing* young adult leaders rather than expecting them to show up fully prepared to lead as well as (or better than) those who've been leading for the past twenty-five years?

Here's one of the most liberating discoveries we've made about cultivating young leaders: *when young adults drop the ball on assignments, it's part of the development process.* It's not proof that they don't have what it takes. It's not a sign that the church should stop giving them leadership opportunities. *It's just normal.*

I know what you're thinking: *So now we're supposed to give young adults leadership so they can drop the ball? Now that's a great leadership development plan!*

The solution is straightforward. If we know that young leaders are likely to drop the ball, we build in more deliberate onboarding and check-in processes along the way. The system set out in chapters eight to fourteen provides a great foundation to not only develop young adults in leadership but also to give older generations a way to walk alongside them during the process.

For now, all you need to know about the system is this: if you want to kill your mission and spike your stress level, expect all young adults to get assignments done on time (or better yet, expect them to come up with the right assignments intuitively!).

Expecting seamless maturity from young adults only serves to reinforce our rationale for keeping them in a holding pattern. Without having the opportunity to actually lead, they're unlikely to stay around long enough to learn the leadership skills the church needs from them.

When it comes to establishing workable, realistic processes for mentoring the next generation into church leadership, the older generations seem to have a follow-through problem too.

Playing Varsity

As a sophomore in high school, my friend Jason got to play on the varsity team for the last game of the season. And by "play" I mean practice with the team and sit on the bench until the last thirty seconds of the game.

Regardless, Jason was elated, and so were we. We stood in the stands going crazy for the last thirty seconds of the blowout. We photocopied his class picture and made makeshift masks of Jason's face that we wore as he stepped onto the court.

We weren't thinking about the outcome of the game. It was a big-time opportunity for our tenth-grade friend, and we were thrilled he had made it.

There's nothing wrong with playing JV, but few athletes set that as their goal. No one starts training for a marathon with the hope of getting halfway there. Young adults today are looking for places to "play varsity."

We have to do better than "let's wait until you're ready."

This year, I got to watch one of our young leaders come alive by being given the chance to play varsity. The step made a profound impact on him *and* produced a twenty thousand dollar savings for the church.

James was working as an intern, helping one of our pastors plant a new church that would hold worship services in a school gymnasium. The team was busy researching and developing an all-in-one portable system, including sound and screen equipment, chairs, coffeepots, and children's classroom equipment. No small task.

James had been working hand in hand with the consulting group charged with helping the church put together the entire system, basically a $150,000 package. Being somewhat of a tech geek with many connections in the audiovisual world, James took a deeper dive into the auditorium design and offered an alternative, working with a local dealer with great connections.

The result?

A savings of almost $20,000, and a couple of unhappy consultants. After James introduced his ideas, the consultants were taken aback, scrambling to figure out how all the pieces might fit together. And frankly, they were more than a little miffed that a twenty-two-year-old had the gumption to push back on their expertise.

What I found most interesting, though, was how James's pastor handled it. Despite pleas from the consulting team, his message was consistent: "James is our representative for this part of the project." James regularly updated him, even recorded some conversations with the consultants, but the pastor repeatedly told James, "I trust you. I think you're doing a great job handling this situation."

This was a big deal for James. "This was a $150,000 decision," he told me. "I've never had such high stakes for anything else in my entire life. But if we're going to spend that kind of money, I really felt passionate about getting the design right."

Sure, the pastor would have stepped in if the whole situation had begun to spiral, but he had the discipline to coach his apprentice without trying to control the particulars of the outcome. When I asked the pastor about his approach, his response was deliberate: "I already know how to navigate something like this; James doesn't. But he'll run into situations like this later on in his life, and here's a golden opportunity to learn how to navigate something like this with a coach alongside him. I wouldn't want to short-circuit that process just because he's young."

When we place young adults in a holding tank, when we place too much importance on making sure they're ready, we rob them of an essential development opportunity. And we miss out on chances to cheer them on, see them succeed (and help them recalibrate when they don't), and prepare them (and our churches) for the future.

Mistake 6

Give Up Too Soon

> *Success is stumbling from failure to failure*
> *with no loss of enthusiasm.*
>
> WINSTON CHURCHILL

> *The rise of the "nones" surely suggests it is the end of religion,*
> *as we know it. Forget churches; forget priests and pastors;*
> *forget the Bible; forget organized religion generally.*
>
> GARY LADERMAN

Back in the days of the American Gold Rush, a man named R. U. Darby saw his uncle caught up in "gold fever," taking off for the West hoping to strike it rich. He staked a claim in Colorado and got busy digging. The work was difficult, the results were minimal, but the dream of riches compelled him not to quit.

One day Darby discovered a vein of gold too big to mine without more equipment. He covered the mine, retraced his footsteps back to Maryland, and told his relatives and a few neighbors about his "strike."

With the help of family and friends, Darby collected enough money for the needed machinery and had it shipped to Colorado. At this point, R. U. Darby joined his uncle to mine the treasure.

As they smelted down the first cartload of ore, the returns revealed that they had discovered one of Colorado's richest mines ever. All they needed to do was keep mining. With high hopes, they continued to drill—until the unexpected happened.

Without warning, the vein of gold ore disappeared. They kept desperately drilling, but no more gold was to be found. Eventually, they sold the machinery for scrap to a junkyard for a few hundred dollars and headed back home.

On a whim, the junkyard owner decided to call in an engineer to look at the old mine. The engineer calculated that the vein could be found again if the miner followed the engineer's instructions, based on specific fault lines.

The junkyard owner went to work exactly as directed and found the lost vein of gold—which turned out to be even larger than predicted—just three feet from where Darby had stopped drilling.

How many of our churches are working hard, drilling in the wrong places, losing heart, and giving up, unaware of where the fault lines are? After the initial excitement at the first few brainstorming meetings, too many churches decide "working with young adults just isn't for us."

I wonder if all the popular research about young adults has actually contributed to the problem.

The Chicken Little Syndrome

With all due respect to the very helpful surveys conducted by the Pew Research Center and others during the last decade or so, I'm afraid the results may be giving us permission to make the most paralyzing mistake of all: giving up altogether.

The American church has begun to accept—even embrace—the doomsday projections about young adults and the church. And with the power of a self-fulfilling prophecy, these results have led too many church leaders to focus their attention anywhere but on young adult ministry.

It's been referred to as the crisis of the "nones," the rising tide of American young adults who check "none" when asked for their religious affiliation. You've likely heard statistics such as these:

> Young people today are not only more religiously unaffiliated than their elders; they are also more religiously unaffiliated than previous generations of young people ever have been as far back as we can tell. This really is something new.[1]

> It is possible that more Millennials who were raised unaffiliated will begin to identify with a religion as they get older, get married, and have children, but previous Pew Research Center studies suggest that generational cohorts typically do not become more religiously affiliated as they get older. And the new survey finds that most generational cohorts actually are becoming less religiously affiliated as they age.[2]

Little hopeful data exists regarding young adults and the church. Almost every study publicized about this generation has the potential effect of motivating us to pack it up, throw in the towel, and hope against hope that a magical resurgence of goodwill toward organized religion will somehow rise up in this generation.

Beyond formal research, most churches have enough firsthand evidence of their own. Many have tried. They've started contemporary services, launched young adult programs, and held focus groups. They've asked successful youth pastors to lead the young adult ministry. And very little has worked.

Like the turkey and goose confronted by Chicken Little's incontrovertible proof that the sky really was falling, most of us have a hard time arguing against an avalanche of evidence. The verdict is in that young adults are out, as far as the church is concerned. When it comes to young adult ministry, I'm afraid the Chicken Little Syndrome is alive and well.

The Cost May Still Be Coming

When I asked the leaders of one church, "What happened to your young adult ministry?" here's what I heard:

* It's too hard to connect with them consistently.

* Our older members are so resistant to change.

* We don't have enough young adults here to make it worth our effort.

This church, by its own admission, used to be a place young adults frequently attended. They had a simple monthly program, young adults in worship leadership, and a good number active in the life of the church. But now, five years later, those young adults are almost totally gone.

I was curious. The pastor explained:

They were mostly a core group of really connected high school and college students who just kept that connection in the following years. They stayed here, and they stayed together. But as they got older, got married, and got full-time jobs (often out of town), they ever so slowly lost their connection to the church. Their connection with each other was the only thing keeping them here, and without it they had no real connection to the church.

"What would have helped them connect beyond their group of peers?" I wondered aloud. His response was fascinating:

A combination of things, I'm sure. But ultimately, I think we just stopped trying to move our church's culture toward them, and we started expecting them to move toward us. We stopped innovating in all of our ministry areas. We stopped asking questions about what that generation was looking for. We ran into enough resistance from older generations to feel like it wasn't really worth the fight. And now they've almost all left.

As we spoke, I could hear the regret in his voice. In fact, we were talking because the church was struggling. They were now a congregation of people mostly age fifty-five and older, with attendance in a downward trend despite the fact that their community was growing.

The pastor admitted, "The community has changed, but we haven't changed with it. It would have been a lot easier to keep our young adults involved than to have to start all over like we're doing now."

On one hand, it's easy to look at your church *today* and say, "We're okay. This just isn't an issue we have time or energy for right now." But churches are never static; they're always moving, growing, shifting, and merging into their next chapters. Too often churches put off making a significant investment in young adult ministry; determining that the startup costs are too high, they give up altogether.

Most churches look at today's financial bottom line, and as long as today's bills are getting paid, they feel little motivation to change. Even in the face of stagnant growth or declining attendance numbers, many churches can reason the challenges away, assuming a temporary lull rather than a trajectory of decline. This pastor's experience can easily be any church's experience.

The Missing Future

When it comes to why it has given up on young adult ministry, each church seems to have its own unique cocktail of excuses:

* We're in the middle of a capital campaign and just can't add one more thing to our plate.

* We don't have the money to hire someone. We're barely keeping the lights on as it is.

* No other churches seem to be reaching this age group. Why should we waste our energy on something no one else is doing?

* They'll come back as soon as they have children.

* We have only two young adults in our whole church, and we hardly ever see *them*.

* Our worship service is too old-fashioned to appeal to young people.

* We must be realistic. Young adults give very little in offerings, and by the time they *do* have money to give, they move to another church or another town.

But our excuses will cost us. Dearly.

Sure, the fact that churches are doing virtually nothing when it comes to young adult ministry is a loss for young adults. But it's an even greater loss for the church.

That's because so much about what drives young adults resonates deeply with the gospel. This generation elected a president who authored *The Audacity of Hope*. Living a life of meaning, a life that makes a difference, profoundly matters to them. They're committed to leaving the world better for their children. Whether it's putting an end to Majority World poverty or bullying on the playground, this generation steadfastly refuses to believe that the status quo has to remain in place.

Trevor Neilson of Global Philanthropy Group says, "61 percent of young adults are worried about the state of the world and feel personally responsible to make a difference."[3] They can make this impact driven by their faith or not, but most will invest their hours, resources, and passion into making a difference somewhere.

It's true. Good young adult ministry will make things messier for a church as it pushes for a faster pace of change. Young adults have little patience with "business as usual." They tend to be impatient with incremental reform, preferring more radical change instead. No wonder most churches are simply annoyed, confused, and frightened by them.

If young adults take a greater leadership role in our churches, they may take us to places we had never planned to go. But consider the alternative.

If we don't allow, invite, and embrace their voices, it will likely cost us even more. Beyond the imminent threat of churches simply going out of business, we'll miss the out-of-left-field kingdom impact that might never happen apart from a partnership with this generation.

Back in 2011, our church almost missed out.

Anna, one of our college students, was home for a semester and volunteering in our church. As time came for her to return to class, she struggled with the inevitable loss of her church community. She hadn't connected with a church near campus and was saddened by the limited options for Christian community on campus.

So her mother presented a ridiculous—yet simple—solution: "I could sit in the front row on Sunday mornings with my laptop and Skype the whole service to you."

That idea sparked something even bigger in Anna. She began thinking, "Out of seven thousand students, there have to be other people on campus looking for the same thing." She latched onto the idea and started putting legs to a dream.

Anna returned to school and gathered a group of friends to pray and dream together. They reserved a lecture hall for Sunday mornings, recruited a few musicians to lead worship, and bought some bagels and coffee. Week after week, they tuned in for a live stream of our Sunday morning sermon, from an actual video camera, not just a video chat recorded on her mom's laptop.

Several weeks after launching, Anna called me, saying, "Last night at 1 a.m., a friend drunk-dialed me and asked if she could come to our church on Sunday morning," which she did. Today that community has grown to more than sixty college students who run the ministry by themselves, passing the reins to a new group of seniors each year.

Our leadership team never would have considered creating a mission to this college ten hours away. If we had waited for this ministry to be part of a top-down strategic plan, it *never* would have happened. But our congregation gave the opportunity to a twenty-year-old who led the way for us to help her make an impact in an unconventional way. This work exceeded all our expectations.

Yes, young adult ministry brings unique challenges. But it also brings unimaginable possibilities for the future of our church. Neil Howe and William Strauss, in their book *Millennials Rising: The Next Great Generation*, take this view:

> As a group, Millennials are unlike any other youth generation in living memory. They are more numerous, more affluent, better educated, and more ethnically diverse. More important, they are beginning to manifest a wide array of positive social habits that older Americans no longer associate with youth, including a new focus on teamwork, achievement, modesty, and good conduct. Only a few years from now, this can-do youth revolution will overwhelm the cynics and pessimists. Over the next decade, the Millennial Generation will entirely recast the image of youth from downbeat and alienated to upbeat and engaged—with potentially seismic consequences for America.[4]

Surprised?

By and large, in my research and interviews, most approaches to young adult ministry boil down to a few random shots in the dark, a vaguely anxious "I sure hope this works" or "I've got a great idea" attitude. Sadly, most churches try a few things, don't see rapid results, and decide (or decide by default), "We don't really *do* young adult ministry. We've tried, but it just doesn't work here."

But young adult ministry won't work anywhere when we "try a few things." You don't grow a tree by dipping the roots in the dirt once every few weeks!

When we stop trying, we cut off the source of possibilities in our future ministry that we couldn't even dream of today. Unfortunately, churches tend to value *stability for today* so much that they stop investing in the very thing that might bring them success in the future. This refusal to work *on* ministry with young adults ends up wasting amazing potential and results in our missing out on young adults such as Rachel.

A Place for Rachel

Rachel, who's in her final year of college, has no upbringing in Christianity and no real reason to believe in God. She's a classic "none" in the Pew Research study.

Last spring, Rachel attended a stage production of the Easter story with some friends from our church. Afterward she asked, "Wait, who is the Judas guy?" She wasn't averse to the church, just unfamiliar with it and its stories. But she's been coming to our church for almost a year now and was recently baptized.

Rachel talks about how thankful she is for "her" church and how often she finds herself in prayer throughout the day. After worship each week, Rachel stands in a circle with a dozen others like her. They talk about the service. They talk about what's happening in their lives. They go to lunch together most weeks.

Young adults are here. They aren't in hiding. They're searching, exploring, and in some places engaging.

At the same time that Rachel's story is unfolding and many other young adults are searching, the church in the United States is losing members, losing focus, losing hope. The church in America needs help.

Enter the next generation.

Researcher Thom Rainer interviewed a young adult named Leslie, who identified with pinpoint accuracy *why* most young adults are frustrated with the church:

> "I'm not antichurch," Leslie explained to me. Leslie grew up in a Christian home. She appreciates her parents' clear convictions and sacrificial service in the church. . . . "But so much of what takes place in my parents' church is just keeping the doors open. Pay the staff. Keep the building nice. And give 10 percent or more of the church's income for someone else to do missions," she told us almost breathlessly.
>
> "But that's plodding Christianity," she continued. "It has no urgency about it. It's more concerned about the people in the church than those outside the church. It breaks my heart that . . . so many churches have members who argue about Robert's Rules of Order or which members will serve on the personnel committee. We just don't have time for such foolishness."[5]

Too many churches have decided that young adult ministry is more trouble than it's worth. They've tried creating new programs, launching new worship styles, expecting young adults to act like predictable consumers—and then they quit when it doesn't work.

We may be mortgaging a bright future for a stable today, missing out on the potentially unimaginable impact these young disciples of Jesus can have on a world in desperate need of God's healing love.

Maybe it's time to try a new approach. Maybe we just need to dig three feet deeper. Maybe we're *that* close to striking gold.

Beyond Fixing

Christianity got over the difficulty of combining furious opposites,
by keeping them both, and keeping them both furious.

G. K. CHESTERTON

Only the arrogant and dogmatic find paradox hard to accept.

RICHARD FOSTER

In 1993, French electrician Emile Leray was stranded in a
Moroccan desert. He was traveling through North Africa when
he was stopped at a military outpost. He was told the area was
restricted and he'd have to turn around. But when the patrol wasn't
looking, Leray put the pedal to the floor and drove into the desert,
avoiding a lengthy detour.

Far from the outpost and twenty miles from the nearest village,
the undercarriage of his car hit a rock, cracking the axle and ren-
dering the vehicle totally inoperable, leaving him stranded.

With limited food and water, Leray considered the simple solutions at hand:

* Start walking? He'd never make it.

* Signal for help? There was no one to see it.

* Fix the car? It was beyond repair.

"I put myself in . . . survival mode," he said. "I ate less; I monitored my supply of water and food to make them last as long as possible." But survival mode could last only so long. He needed a different set of options, a different solution, and he needed it quick. Against all hope, Leray did something remarkable.

He didn't walk to safety.

He wasn't rescued.

He didn't repair the car.

Leray spent twelve days disassembling the car and reassembling it into a makeshift motorcycle that he could ride to safety. He asked a different question—because questions such as, "How can I fix the car?" or, "How can I make the water last longer?" would only delay inevitable death. Instead, he started asking, "What if?"

A New Conversation

It's time for us to start asking different, unexpected questions about young adult ministry:

* What if we stop trying to pull young adults back and instead follow where *they're* going?

* What if we invite them to lead the church into its next chapter?

* What if we dare to believe there's more to their story than we're telling ourselves today?

It might be easy to assume that the solution to the problem of young adult ministry is to simply *quit making mistakes*, particularly the ones identified in the first half of this book, or maybe even *fix the mistakes we've already made*.

Naming our most common missteps is, of course, a fine starting point. But a focus on *not* doing the *wrong* things won't get us out of the desert. Instead, we must build something entirely new, reassembling the problem into the solution.

The next eight chapters offer a way to think differently about reaching this generation of young adults and college students. To get there, we need to travel down the path of paradox.

The Six Paradoxical Priorities

As you likely know well, young adults are often defined by unpredictability and paradox. They want high incomes but are resistant to sacrificing the *life* side of the work-life balance. They prioritize meaningful work *and* a comfortable lifestyle. They seek honesty and regular feedback from their managers, but many don't want to become managers themselves.

Whatever solutions we develop to the young adult problem will require the church to lean into the very nature of young adults and provide a paradoxical response.

Here's a quick refresher: a *paradox* is a statement that seemingly contradicts itself or a combination of two statements that seem to oppose each other. For example:

* A card says on one side, "The sentence on the other side of this card is true." On the other side, "The sentence on the other side of this card is false."

* Can God make a rock so big even God can't lift it?

* Pinocchio tells you, "My nose will now grow."

* The phrase "Ignore all the rules" is a rule itself.

To the typical either-or question, the quintessential young adult will answer yes!

One author puts it this way: "Millennials have been taught to see the back story, that every upside has a downside, so they often want to balance two contradictory things to get its upside while minimizing its downside. They want both."[1] Young adults live in a world of the both-and. They live in a world of paradox, and embracing paradox might be the key to reaching them.

Christians have, of course, long embraced paradox. H. Richard Niebuhr describes it well in *Christ and Culture*: "In Christ all things have become new, and yet everything remains as it was from the beginning. God has revealed Himself in Christ, but hidden Himself in His revelation; the believer knows the One in whom he has believed, yet walks by faith, not sight."[2]

We receive life through death, gain through loss, honor through humility, power through meekness. Our faith inhales and exhales with the breath of paradox. I love that G. K. Chesterton reportedly said that, in Christianity, we don't just have doxology so much as *paradox*ology.

As we unpack the second half of this book, I'll introduce you to six paradoxical priorities that offer stepping stones to a thriving ministry with young adults.

Here's a quick summary:

Paradox 1. Succeed by being willing to fail. One of our biggest roadblocks to success with young adult ministry is our own paralyzing fear of failure. It keeps us stuck doing the same ineffective things again and again, unable to find the kinds of ministry that will work for fear of working through the things that don't. Young adults are taking the reins of leadership out into the world, and to effectively reach them in the church we need to find ways of giving them the keys and letting them drive us into the future. But that means we must take a different view of failure and embrace the trial-and-error nature of building a ministry *with* young adults instead of *for* them. Churches that begin to pursue repeated failure with young adults might find themselves stumbling into more and more success.

Paradox 2. Focus on young adults by taking the focus off young adults. Our most common reaction to the need for young adult ministry is to paint a target squarely on the backs of young adults and pour our money, time, and resources into attracting them with every trick (mistake) we can think of. But if we really want to attract young adults, we need to be crystal clear about the *church's* mission. The more we focus on reaching our communities and our world, and the more effective we are at doing it, the more interested young adults will be in joining. We must think mission first *then* young adults.

Paradox 3. Reach young people by gathering more old people. To really reach young adults, our goal needs to be bigger than trying to gather large numbers of them into a group. To build a sustainable young adult ministry, you'll need a team of older adults working to deliberately connect with young adults. It takes a "village of gurus" to build the kind of ministry you want, recognizing the deep desire of many young adults to be mentored and connected to older generations. We must see young adult ministry as a team sport, not as work to be done by any single individual.

Paradox 4. Reach one young adult at a time through a system to reach them all. We've already talked a lot about the priority of making individual, relational connections with young adults. But your ministry will never stand up under pressure without systems and structures to undergird it. These systems ensure that your singular initiatives sustain their impact over time, continuing to build greater and greater momentum.

Paradox 5. Respond to lack of commitment by asking for more. Young adults aren't devoid of options in their lives. The world is at their fingertips more than ever before. Perhaps that's why many people see young adults as scattered, unfocused, and seemingly unable to keep their commitments. As a result, the typical church responds by providing more options and lower expectations. But as counterintuitive as it might seem, churches gain more traction with young adults by asking for *more* commitment. Strangely, the young adult who has no time for a thirty-minute, optional Bible study actually might give ten hours a week to a compelling vision they believe in. Our mission is to make sure we invite young adults into missions that matter, not thinly veiled marketing schemes designed to get them to attend.

Paradox 6. Attract young adults to your church by sending them away. One of the most difficult aspects of working with young adults is the reality that, because of career shifts, life transitions, or wanderlust, many won't stick around forever. Rather than fight against their transient nature, we can build ministries that embrace this very quality and develop ways of doing ministry that aren't thrown off course by young adult transience. The best ministry with young adults happens when we equip them for life beyond our church even if they do stay.

Maybe by this point your head is starting to hurt. But I hope you'll hang in there for these next few chapters as we walk the path of paradox together. All along that road are young adults hungering for an authentic life in Christ, even when they express that longing in ways we don't exactly expect.

The facts don't lie:

> There are the thousands of young adults who gather at Urbana every other year, the 20,000 who gathered in Kansas City for the International House of Prayer's One Thing gathering, and the 40,000 college students at Passion Conferences. These events instill confidence that the next generation of leaders loves Jesus and is passionate about serving Him and making Him known among their generation. Not all of these worshippers are showing up at church on Sunday morning—at least, in this period of their lives—but their passion for God still burns strong.[3]

Our solution to establishing thriving young adult ministries pushes beyond traditional either-or patterns and easy-answer thinking. Let's begin down a paradoxical path designed for *any* church to implement.

Our car may have broken down and left us with little hope, but there's a way out of the desert. Just keep reading.

Paradox 1

Succeed by Being Willing to Fail

We are all failures—at least the best of us are.

J. M. BARRIE

Everything stinks till it's finished.

DR. SEUSS

On a recent flight, I shuffled down the cramped aisle, stuffed my oversized bag into the undersized bin, and found my seat for the next two hours. That's when I noticed it.

A dropdown TV was playing an extended commercial for the Hard Rock Cafe. For five straight minutes, a story unfolded about all the good work the restaurant chain is doing around the world. This advertisement wasn't simply about reducing, reusing, and re-cycling. It was about digging wells in Africa, adopting orphans from South America, and rescuing polar bears in the arctic. Not a single mention of the menu!

And not one person in the ad looked a day over twenty-five. It ended with the tagline "Hard Rock Cares."

Later that week, my wife and I went to the movies. As we munched popcorn and anticipated previews, a Pepsi commercial played with thirty talking heads sharing stories of the positive impact they're making in the world.

Again, not a single person over twenty-five. The tagline? "Every generation refreshes the world."

Like no previous generation, young adults believe they can make a deep, long-lasting, positive impact in this world. Even the work of organizations such as Hard Rock Cafe and Pepsi draws on this inner drive of today's young adults.

"Secular" culture is vastly outpacing the church in equipping young adults to do good. Too often the church tries to attract young adults to meetings with pizza and *Amazing Race* scavenger hunts. Or more likely, we expect them to show up, sit in a chair, and listen (and then wonder in amazement why they don't come—or even particularly want to).

It's time to face a sobering reality: corporate marketers may have a bigger vision for young adults than the church does. Savvy companies understand the topics and issues that motivate young adults to buy their products. What if a bigger vision exists for this generation than how they can become consumers of the church?

In the church, we know how to do what we know how to do. And even though we may no longer have any reasonable purpose for continuing in the same direction, we keep doing what we know how to do, even when it doesn't work. So instead of trying something new and stepping into the Netflix, on-demand world of young adults, most churches complain that people just aren't committed enough to engage our ministries the way we want them to.

One huge roadblock to innovating with young adults is that we'll have to try things that sometimes won't work—something most churches try hard to avoid.

In short, to succeed we'll have to fail. With young adult ministry, most churches would rather "succeed" at doing what doesn't work than risk failing at what might. Meanwhile, companies such as Hard Rock Cafe and Pepsi are outpacing the church by taking risks and serving up new approaches instead of just burgers and sodas.

This chapter encourages you and your team to consider investing at least some energy into creating space for experimentation and invention. You'll learn about Kid President, hackathons, and why we need to stop adding young adults to our churches. I'll provide a window into the mindset that's required for any church hoping to do more than polish tired programs that have little promise of producing the desired results.

You'll be asked to embrace a mindset of innovation, creativity, and, yes, failure. When it comes to ministry with young adults, if at first you don't succeed, you're probably doing it right.

The Untapped Missional Heartbeat

Any church hoping to build a long-lasting ministry with young adults must invest in *their* desire to change the world. Without it, Do not pass Go. Do not collect $200.

For young adults, making a mark on the world is a key intersection (some might say *the* key intersection) of their world and their faith. By and large, young adults won't engage for long in a church that isn't helping them engage in that mission.

But their passion for investing in new enterprises won't always be comfortable for us. I learned this painful lesson a few years ago.

In October 2010, our church launched its third campus. I'd known this season was coming but was taken aback by how many of our core group of young adults left for the new campus. This wasn't a church split or a conflict with the pastor. It was a healthy birth. But our people seemed relieved, even eager, to depart!

As the pastor who stayed behind at the "old" church, I felt abandoned. Of course, I understood rationally that the rapid departure had nothing to do with what was wrong with me (though there's plenty!). It had everything to do with the opportunity young adults saw to make an impact for Christ in a new community.

Young people's missional hearts long for more than random acts of kindness once a month. Raking leaves for the elderly this month and working at the soup kitchen next month are fine. But by themselves, they don't tap into the deep young-adult longing to make an impact.

I've learned something extremely valuable about how the typical young adult approaches church: *If we're not trying to change the world, then what's the point?*

A top reason so few young adults are engaged in churches is because those congregations offer so little in the way of opportunities for young adults to actually change their world. Without a connection to a missional heartbeat in the church, young adults almost always move on to another church or to a more nimble organization aligned with their passions.

Some churches are trying, but most often they're trying by doing polished-up service projects. Why? Because that's what we know how to do!

According to one study of the (very few) churches doing *anything* focused on young adults, 38 percent say they're doing community service projects.[1] Though 38 percent may not seem like a large number, this is far and away the most common program most churches offer young adults.

Service certainly isn't a bad place to start. But when churches limit the missional engagement of young adults to one-off service projects, these episodic acts of compassion have little stickiness—to the church or to each other.

A huge untapped opportunity remains.

The young adult heart beats with an irrepressible desire to change the world. Young adults are inspired by the broad-reaching impact of a person such as Katie Davis, described this way by Brad Lomenick in *The Catalyst Leader*:

> In 2007, at nineteen years old, Katie Davis traveled to Uganda to teach kindergarten at an orphanage. And she stayed.
>
> Today, she runs an orphanage and a child-sponsorship program that provides hundreds of children with education, food, medical care, and Christian discipleship. The founder of Amazima Ministries, Katie . . . adopted fourteen Ugandan children as her own. It would have been easier for Katie to finish college and pursue the American dream, but God had something better in store for her.[2]

Of course, Davis isn't average, as if there were such a thing among young adults. But make no mistake: the impulse that drove her into her mission is part and parcel of the young adult DNA. Although young adults may not have the words to ask for it, they long for a church that gets them *out* of the church and into the world.

When young adults discover that your church is serious about helping *them* change the world, they'll pay attention. When they're given agency to make an impact rather than just "help out at the church" as volunteers, real engagement begins.

And of course, as you start changing the world together, your church will be changed too.

The New Question

When you start working through the process outlined in this book, there's a good chance someone on your team will wonder: *okay, I'm starting to get it. But when will any of this cause young adults to stream into our sanctuary and become good members?*

It may be time to ask an entirely different question.

As long as our first focus is on getting young adults into our buildings to attend our programs as spectators, we reduce the church to one more institution competing for their time and attention; one more place trying to persuade them (with anemic, almost nonexistent marketing); one more place trying to get them to consume something.

We must learn new ways of doing ministry. In other words, we're going to have to fail. This work is too important to simply succeed at what we're comfortable doing. It's too important for us *not* to be willing to fail.

Forbes magazine recently asked, "In the near future millennials will occupy every consequential leadership position in the world, be it in business, academia, government, or in the non-profit sector. Will they be ready to lead?"[3]

The article's assumed answer is "not likely." This is the new question for businesses, for academic institutions, for government. And it should be a huge question on every church's mind as well.

Young adults won't be prepared to lead because we've done so little to create processes that invite and receive their leadership in a way that neither blows up the church nor sends them screaming into the night. Too often the best we've done has been to assemble young adults to ask for input about what kind of program they'd like the church to create for them. The new question is *not* about young adults having more ownership over programs or getting more buy-in to the church's young adult ministry.

Perhaps the most glaring need for young adults in the church is helping them invent and catalyze ministry that isn't primarily for *them*. This involves accessing their passion, creativity, and leadership for a mission larger than themselves or a young adult program. And though I'm talking about the next generation in particular, I hope these same principles continue driving the church's ministry to younger generations for decades to come.

To meet this need, we must let young adults lead in some uncharted areas.

Consider this research by the leadership-development company Virtuali: Among young adults currently in the workforce (ages eighteen to thirty-five), 50 percent are *already* in leadership positions. Half of young adults have a leadership voice in their jobs *right now*. Research also shows that 64 percent felt unprepared when entering their leadership role but (get this!) 41 percent *already* have at least four employees reporting directly to them. Leadership isn't on the future horizon for young adults in America; it's already here. For young adults, leadership is the new trend.[4]

Consider this: When asked about their career and life goals, 70 percent of young adults say they want to launch their own organizations.[5] They're less interested in running someone else's, especially one known for moving at the glacially slow pace of the church.

Young adults are highly motivated to run with dreams of their own. In the corporate world, they aren't waiting around and paying their dues until someone gives them a voice at the table. They already have a voice. When they come to church expecting to have a similar influence, young adults have little patience for the grinding complexity of decision making. Often, as a result, they choose to expend their missional energies elsewhere.

But what if the church provided . . .

A Space to Make the World Awesome

You've probably seen young Robby Novak on YouTube. You may never have learned his name, but you (and a few million others) know him as Kid President, the pint-sized motivational speaker who challenges viewers to "make the world more awesome."

From this section's subheading, maybe you assumed you'd be reading about constructing a physical space conducive to young adult ministry, maybe with a coffee bar complete with fair-trade coffee, like Starbucks for Jesus. But we're talking about a different kind of space.

What if churches created laboratory space for young adults, and what if those young adults were invited to experiment with ways to "make the world more awesome" and, ultimately, invent the church of the future?

This is exactly the kind of challenge many young adults want to sink their teeth into. For those in (*and* outside) the church, banding together with a community of people to contribute to a cause bigger than themselves strikes a resonant chord. Though the examples of this primal entrepreneurial urge among young adults are legion, the following are a few reminders.

* An astounding 62 percent of young adults define themselves as innovative people.[6]

* The nonprofit Food Recovery Network (founded and run by young adults and featured on MSNBC) has created a self-sustaining system for college students, universities, and businesses to work together to save otherwise-wasted food to feed the hungry.[7]

* Boyan Slat was only in high school when he proposed a machine with movable arms to collect plastic trash in the ocean. Now, with support from the government and a report detailing the project's feasibility, the Dutch inventor has raised *more than $2 million* to make The Ocean Cleanup a reality. Slat says it can help remove half of the Great Pacific Garbage Patch (roughly the size of Texas) in a decade.[8]

* Billions of people around the world suffer from tooth decay because dental care isn't affordable. Five University of Pennsylvania undergraduates developed a tasty solution: Sweet Bites. The FDA-approved chewing gum contains xylitol, a natural sugar substitute that can reverse and prevent tooth decay. The

gum launched in July in Bangalore, India, and is now being produced locally.[9]

Young adults want to lead, and they want to build something new that makes an impact. But the sad truth is that the church is the last place most of them think of when they're looking for opportunities to do something catalytic, dynamic, and innovative.

In the economic marketplace, companies are valued, at least in part, by how much they spend on research and development (R & D). Companies that invest in innovative methods to improve existing products and services or in dreaming up entirely new revenue streams are simply more valuable than companies that don't.

Where, I wonder, has the church's R & D department been? For the most part, admittedly, it's been virtually nonexistent.

What if young adult ministry were to become the R & D department of every thriving church in America? What if, when young adults—inside or outside the church—dreamed of changing the world, their first thought was, *I have to find a church to help me with this*?

Unfortunately, to many young adults, the church is like a first-generation iPad. Maybe you know what I mean.

Last week our church finally retired the original, first-generation iPad we'd been using to run some lighting. At that time, the device was less than five years old and it was already out of date.

Nothing is physically *wrong* with the tablet; it works fine. Not a scratch on it. I can use it to connect to Wi-Fi and check my email without a problem. But the operating system no longer has the capacity to receive the latest updates, and most new applications won't work on it.

It's easy to feel frustrated that a company would make something with such a short shelf life that I have to buy a new version when the old one still works. But it's really not the manufacturer's fault.

The community—that's us—decided to create (and use) new applications and operating systems that go beyond what we could do previously. We innovated. We moved forward. We waited in line for the new device with the updated operating system. The manufacturer didn't do that; we did.

A typical young adult might say: "Nothing's wrong with the church. It still works fine. But the applications I need for my life are different from a generation ago—so different, in fact, that the church might be a mostly useless artifact. Sure, I can still go there to sing hymns and sit in a class, but that's not exactly how I want to spend my time."

Although most churches consider this situation a crisis, few are taking the time to see the undeniable opportunity buried right beneath the presenting challenge:

Young adults are drawn to the process of innovating, beta testing, and connecting the dots to make the world better. However, almost no faith communities are providing a space where young adults can develop something new.

The church—of every generation but particularly this one—desperately needs fresh expressions of what church can be, with new operating systems and applications. Young adults aren't only eager; they have the skills to actually help the church discover new ways of experiencing life and mission together.

Sadly, traditional church leadership often feels totally unprepared to do much more than keep the lights on and the services running on time. What would happen if the ordinary church created a space where young adults—both those connected to it and those not yet connected—could work side by side to "make the world more awesome"? What would happen if churches began seeing young adults' missional longings as a doorway into the church and stopped relying on food and fellowship programs?

Let me state the obvious: very few of us, especially among young adults, get passionate about being on a committee whose primary function is maintaining the status quo. Having a voice (or even a vote) isn't enough.

More and more young adults get excited about hacking away at a glaring social problem, which our world provides in ample supply. They want to do something to move the needle and are willing to make sacrificial steps to do so. It's no surprise that at a Passion Conference a few years ago, a group of college students (who, by definition, "have no money," right?) raised more than four million dollars to help end human trafficking.

What the Hack?

As we begin talking through the practicalities of creating a laboratory for innovation in your congregation (a helpful process for starting one can be found in "Change-the-World Missional Laboratory Launch Plan" online at ivpress.com/sustainable-young-adult-ministry), I want to introduce you to a term I learned a few years ago: *hacking*.

Though easily confused for the kind of work done by nefarious cybercriminals, hacking is an increasingly popular approach to solving society's problems.

It's become more and more common for universities, businesses, and governments to invite bright, creative, tech-savvy young adults to spend a day, a weekend, or even a week to a collaborative, sometimes competitive, "hackathon" to solve an intractable social issue. Many now extend invitations to more than the technologically gifted, welcoming creative thinkers with a variety of gifts.

The following are a couple of examples.

* One municipality sponsored a hackathon to solve the city's chronic pothole problem.[10]

* A group of venture capitalists sponsored a competition for hackers to solve challenges as far-flung as organizing pet medical records, creating a social platform to connect cooperative farmers and their customers, and reducing the duplication of social services in the city.[11]

What would happen if instead of trying to polish our young adult websites to attract young adults to more meetings, churches identify a big need in the community that aligns with the calling of the church and gather young adults to try to develop solutions? And what if we provide collaborative coaches from a variety of generations and disciplines and put a young adult or two in charge? Could this approach fail? Possibly. But it also might create a new kind of energy with the next generation that churches aren't experiencing right now.

Don't miss this: not only is hacking in the DNA of young adults, it's also a fundamental impulse of the Christian church called to be a missional community on the move. In God's hilarious economy, hacking young adults may be exactly what the declining church of today needs, and together the church must take some risks.

More and more Christian young adults are cooking up all kinds of outside-the-box ideas—hymn sings at breweries, businesses that employ the unemployed, and more incarnations of coffeehouses than I can count (see ministryincubators.com). Once we understand the widespread appeal of participating in a change-the-world project, we begin to get a picture of the currency that holds the most value for so many young adults.

Sure, these groups might come up with lots of ideas that will never work. Failure is inherent to any successful laboratory. But the process of creation and innovation itself—including the rhythm of experimentation, failure, prototype, failure, beta test, failure— can become a catalyst for rich community and a magnetic doorway into young adult discipleship.

Noah's Dream

Noah was a longtime young adult friend of mine. We volunteered together, played cards together, and I even helped him paint his house. He was a small-business owner, running a tech company he started and managed. But eventually Noah felt a call to something different, so he sold his business in order to pursue ministry. He enrolled in seminary, planning to put his business skills forever on the shelf.

After graduation, Noah joined a congregation interested in church planting. He was excited to tackle a role as a staff pastor at this growing church with an eye to planting their next one.

But, as is often the case with young adults, Noah's story didn't follow a linear course. Something in him just wouldn't let him keep his business savvy out of his ministry. He assumed he'd be using his startup business experience to plant a church, but he encountered an unexpected opportunity that combined ministry and business.

While looking for a location for a church plant, Noah came across a piece of property for sale. As he built friendships in the neighborhood he learned that it lacked a gathering place. With fear and trembling, Noah suggested that instead of building a traditional church structure, the congregation build a combination coffee shop and tap house, serving home-brewed coffee and craft-brewed beer.

Astoundingly, when the church leadership heard about Noah's idea for this space, they were all-in. Within a year, his sponsoring church had purchased the property, scrapped their plans for a new traditional campus, bought the building, paid for renovations, and invested time, energy, prayer, and sweat equity in launching this venture. Believe it or not, they even redesigned the entire organizational structure to make room for *more* ventures like it as an expression of their fundamental commitment to engage the community.

Noah's dream didn't start out as the church's dream, but leadership made the clear choice to invest in it, and it became *their* dream too.

Maybe It's Time to Start Multiplying the Treasure

Both Matthew and Luke record Jesus' often-quoted parable of the talents, the story of a master who, while on a journey, leaves his money in the hands of servants. When the master arrives home to find his investment has multiplied in the hands of some servants, he replies, "Well done, good and faithful servant! You have been faithful with a few things; I will put you in charge of many things. Come and share your master's happiness!" (Matthew 25:21).

However, when the master learns that one servant has buried the gold for safekeeping, the response is, "You wicked, lazy servant! . . . You should have put my money on deposit with the bankers, so that when I returned I would have received it back with interest" (vv. 26-27).

"Well done, good and faithful servant" is a familiar phrase. We hear it often at funerals or when talking about our reward in heaven. It's spoken as a comfort to the loved ones of people who have faithfully followed Christ for many years.

Actually, I find those words less than comforting.

This parable is fiercely challenging. According to Jesus, people who simply take care of and protect (some might call this practice "stewardship") what they've been given will hear "you wicked, lazy servant."

Only those who *multiply* the kingdom will hear "well done, good and faithful servant." Not addition. Multiplication. Jesus wants to receive an exponential return on his investment in the church. The math is, well, irrefutable.

Most churches are trying like crazy to *add* more young adults to their ranks. So we focus on programs and promotions in an effort to get a few more in the door. But usually we avoid taking risks, pursuing innovation, or stepping anywhere close to outside the box. What if, instead, we created a dedicated R & D space in our churches for young adults to dream, experiment, and innovate?

Without a commitment to failure, our churches aren't likely to see positive change. Without a mandate to try something that probably won't work, we may never find the things that will. This book offers a number of new approaches to viewing ministry through the lens of paradox. The first paradox is that we'll succeed with young adults only when we're willing to fail. Without this fundamental shift, we may be burying, rather than multiplying, the treasure Jesus has given us.

Paradox 2

Focus on Young Adults by
Taking the Focus off Young Adults

> *If you want to build a ship, don't drum up people together*
> *to collect wood and don't assign them tasks and work, but*
> *rather teach them to long for the endless immensity of the sea.*
>
> ANTOINE DE SAINT-EXUPÉRY

> *I am always wary of decisions made hastily. I am always wary*
> *of the first decision, that is, the first thing that comes*
> *to my mind if I have to make a decision. This is usually*
> *the wrong thing. I have to wait and assess, looking deep*
> *into myself, taking the necessary time.*
>
> POPE FRANCIS

You may feel a little confused at this point, wondering how any of this information will get a single new young adult to stay in your church. If you have doubts, suspend your judgment for a few more chapters.

Here I'll begin introducing you to a slow, sometimes tedious approach that actually works rather than a simple, impulsive one that almost never does.

I confess that I love impulsive buying. I see something, I want it, and too often I buy it.

I go shopping with no intention of buying a thing. Then a sweater (on sale, of course) appears in my bag. Maybe you go grocery shopping and end up buying at least seventeen items that weren't on your list. Or, like a friend of mine, you walk into Home Depot to buy light bulbs and walk out with a riding lawn mower sophisticated enough to groom a PGA green. Whether or not you're an impulsive buyer like me, I'll bet you know exactly what I'm talking about.

Many churches have the exact same problem with young adult ministry. We enter the checkout lane, see racks full of quick and easy solutions for getting young adults in the church, and decide we *must have* them!

We respond to the challenge of young adults in the church (okay, mostly *out of* the church) by throwing ourselves into the first thing we can think of. We get a new logo, throw out a hashtag, or become active on social media. Maybe we switch to fair-trade coffee or hold a worship concert geared especially to young adults (bonus points for using a Hillsong-only set list).

But these kinds of shotgun attempts almost never create the fundamental change required for sustainable young adult ministry. Launching a thriving ministry begins when we change our orientation from doing programs *for* young adults to creating structures to work *with* them, when our imaginations are captured by *their* God-size dreams. But to make this shift, we need a laser focus on something *beyond* young adults themselves.

Shoes and Glasses

A contributor to *Forbes* magazine describes the profound, attractional power that *mission*—the drive to improve the world—has on young adults:

> I have a Millennial-aged friend who only wears Toms shoes despite the fact these shoes hurt his feet, cannot be worn in the rain or cold, and fall apart within weeks, simply because he strongly believes in its mission of providing shoes to third-world children. Essentially, Toms' values and charitable mission override his common sense. And my friend isn't alone in spending his money at companies that do good over ones that offer good products.[1]

Though there's plenty of debate about the real social impact (or harm) of a missional marketing strategy such as the one used by Toms, there's little doubt that this approach resonates deeply with today's young adults. Could we be spending a lot of failed energy, time, and money trying to make a better shoe for young adults, hoping to entice them with our better product instead of supercharging the missional impact we already have?

Although some young adults certainly are less intentional about their buying choices, it's undeniable that young adults have a strong attraction to organizations with a focus on doing good. In fact, according to Horizon Media's "Finger on the Pulse" study, more than eight in ten young adults (81 percent) actually *expect* companies to make a public commitment to good corporate citizenship.[2]

It's time the church woke up to a reality that even *for-profit* companies are embracing: focusing on a mission automatically gets more interest from young adults. By comparison, most young adults see the church as a black hole that diverts money that might otherwise help people and uses it to maintain buildings and programs for its own members. To many young adults, church feels more like a self-serving country club that protects the status quo than an instrument for meaningful social change.

Churches that focus on recruiting and attracting young adults to increase attendance miss the fact that many young adults are significantly more attracted to opportunities to make an impact than to programs designed exclusively for them.

Many young adults are attracted to jobs at the Warby Parker eyeglass company. The reason? Cofounder and CEO Dave Gilboa reports the biggest reason young adults flock to his company is because of its focus on social mission.

For every pair of glasses Warby Parker sells, it delivers one to someone in need, and anyone who works for the company at least three years gets flown somewhere in the world to help administer eye exams and deliver glasses. A company exec confirms, "Having a prominent social mission helps us attract and retain these young, passionate employees."[3]

Maybe you've heard of the beer company that links the sale of its commemorative glassware to the mission of supplying clean water to Africa. Because mission matters to young adults, companies are learning that mission sells to them as well. But the church—with an unparalleled mission vision built into its very DNA—seems to have missed this point altogether, promoting instead warmed-up programs that look similar to what worked so well twenty to fifty years ago.

Beyond Prostituting Mission

I hope you're ready to press the pause button.

Sure, an increasing focus on mission is central to attracting more and more young adults, but we must walk a careful tightrope when it comes to mission.

A ministry mentor once told me, "Never prostitute a friendship. Never build a relationship for the sake of some other goal, even a good goal like getting them to come to your church or even make a decision for Christ. Love people because God loves them. Never try to leverage the relationship for something else."

That's a wise warning.

The same could be said about engaging with mission for the purpose of attracting young adults. Do we feed starving children in Africa because it makes us feel good? Do we run a community-service day primarily to enhance our church's reputation in the city? Do we lean into our missional values so young adults will be attracted to *our* church more than the church down the street?

Mission, in and of itself, must come before young adults, it must not be a clever tool for getting them engaged or to sell them on our church. We engage in mission first and foremost because it's at the heart of what it means to be a disciple of Jesus.

Young adults are attracted to churches that engage *authentically* in mission, not as a means to simply grow membership. The call to live missionally can never be reduced to a marketing strategy. It's at the core of any faithful church. The good news is that our call to engage young adults may actually have the effect of calling the church back to an appropriate focus on mission beyond its own walls.

Many churches may have a written vision statement that prominently highlights mission. But their *functional* mission statement, the one they really live by, the one demonstrated in their week-to-week priorities, is "avoid failure at all cost by continuing business as usual." This is the kind of church the typical young adult wants to avoid at all cost.

When the church stands silent in the face of injustice, this generation tunes out. Young adults expect to see the church tip the scales of its focus toward a compelling mission.

When young adults—even deeply committed followers of Christ—don't see a missional focus in the church, they look elsewhere to engage in a mission with the potential to change the world. And more often than not, they've come to believe that Toms and Warby Parker have a more faithful strategy for changing the world than the church does.

A New Center

By now you've gotten the message: most churches are organizing their young adult ministries around the wrong center. The unquestioned goal (whether assumed or announced publicly) is to get young adults to show up to our buildings or our programs and maybe even persuade them to give, volunteer, or join the church. We want them to listen to us teach and apply our wisdom to their lives.

We want young adults to experience God's presence, walk more fully in the abundant life of Christ, and leave with a passion to impact their world. And we assume, quite logically, that our first step toward this goal is to get them to simply show up to our meetings. But before too long, the organizing marker of a successful young adult ministry becomes getting young people to show up every seven days.

I'm actually grateful for the ways the "nones" are waking up the church by their lack of attendance. But organizing young adult ministry around attendance is a dead end.

Missional church experts are helping us develop a different organizing center: "A missional church is simply any church that organizes itself around the mission of God in this world."[4]

As we reimagine young adult ministry, what if we spent less time trying to get them back into our pews and more time inviting them to join in God's mission? What if we took the focus off young adults and put it on a mission in which they can engage side by side with us?

When I say "invite them to join in God's mission," I'm *not* talking about inviting young adults to a long series of meetings to help the church write (or rewrite) its mission statement. I'm not talking about inviting them to volunteer to help with the church's youth ministry.

I'm talking about starting beyond our own walls. Before we redouble our frantic efforts to get young adults "in here," let's make sure our church is living out the call of Christ *out there*.

Here's the odd and delightful paradox: when we faithfully focus on our *out there* mission first, we stand the greatest chance of seeing young adults worshiping alongside us. It's as if Jesus knew what he was talking about when he said, "Seek first his kingdom and his righteousness, and all these things will be given to you as well" (Matthew 6:33).

Young adults who become partners in mission are much more likely to find mentors in the church and *then* create *their own* young-adult-specific programs.

Beyond the Dots

Figure 10.1. Puzzle of the nine dots

At some point, you've probably seen the puzzle of the nine dots. It goes like this: try to connect all nine dots in figure 10.1 by using only four consecutive lines. Try it.

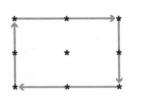

Figure 10.2. First possible attempt at solving the puzzle

If you're like me and thousands of other rookie puzzlers, you'll struggle, believing the solution is found *within* the square shape of the dots. Perhaps something like figure 10.2.

Or maybe like figure 10.3.

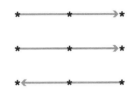

Figure 10.3. Second possible attempt at solving the puzzle

The solution to this puzzle (like the solution to young adult ministry) can be found only when we expand our focus beyond the self-imposed boundaries of what we *expect* the answer to look like.

Try this solution: start at the top left corner and go right, one squares' length beyond the dot. From there, take a diagonal down and back to the left, go straight up and then diagonal down and to the right (see fig. 10.4).

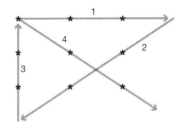

Figure 10.4. Solution to solving the puzzle

Young adult ministry that works makes the focus larger than programs for young adults themselves. There's a solution, but not if we stay limited within the boundaries of programming *for* them.

A New Kind of Softball

I was talking with a young adult couple who had started their church's softball team the previous summer. The wife laughed, "It was the only way I could get him to come to church. Softball is his *thing.*"

For those of us who've been in the church all our lives, especially those over forty, we imagine softball as something the church members do for fellowship, not as a doorway into the life of the church. Most of us see mission the same way—something the people *already in the church* do to bless the community or the world.

But that's not how young adults see it.

When it comes to young adults, particularly those outside the church, mission has become their *thing*. Mission may be the new "softball team" for young adults, a low-threshold doorway into a church community that gives them a chance to do mission collaboratively with all types of people from a variety of generations.

Embrace the paradox: we do our most focused work with young adults when we take our first focus off young adults and align our ministry to a mission that changes the world around us with the gospel of Jesus.

Paradox 3

Reach Young People by
Gathering More Old People

> *I have no question that when you have a team,*
> *the possibility exists that it will generate magic,*
> *producing something extraordinary, a collective creation*
> *of previously unimagined quality or beauty.*
> *But don't count on it.*

J. RICHARD HACKMAN, HARVARD UNIVERSITY

> *You can do what I cannot do. I can do what you cannot do.*
> *Together we can do great things.*

MOTHER TERESA

A few years ago, I read a *Sports Illustrated* article that clarified once and for all the world's most dangerous sport. The headline caught my attention and made me wonder, *Is it football? Rugby? Maybe ultramarathoning?*

Nope.

The most dangerous sport, the one with the highest propensity for injury, is (are you ready for this?) *cheerleading.*

That's right. Cheerleading.

Andrea Atkins observes, "Cheerleading is the most dangerous sport of all, according to the most recent report from the National Center for Catastrophic Sports Injury Research at the University of North Carolina, accounting for half of all catastrophic injuries to female athletes."[1]

For some of you, I know that's shocking. Your daughter was right when she told her brother it was harder to be on the cheerleading squad than to play football.

Cheerleading is no longer just about memorizing cheers, shouting in cadence, and waving pompoms. Routines include tossing a human as high as twenty feet into the air and (hopefully) catching her.

Say what you want about whether cheerleading is a real sport or not, but I've never seen anyone throw a point guard ten feet *above* the hoop in the Final Four!

When it comes to ministry with young adults, the most challenging part isn't planning the program or Bible study. It's not promoting events, making phone calls, or even getting young people to show up. It just may be cheerleading.

Let me explain.

Young adults desperately need a team of people around them who don't do the work *for* them but who inspire, who cheer young adults into work *they're* called to do. And like cheerleading, it's much harder than we might think.

The Numbers 8 Principle

Young adults desperately *want* relationships with older generations. We know the immense formative power these relationships can have on the young, the old, and the entire church. But facilitating these connections can be one of the most difficult tasks of ministry.

It all begins, at least in my mind, with a shift in mindset for the older generation, a shift that can be a bit unsettling. This shift takes us back to a little-known principle God prescribes for passing along leadership. It's buried in Numbers 8, tucked inside a lengthy list of instructions for the Levites, Israel's priestly tribe. The passage could be easy to ignore:

> The LORD said to Moses, "This applies to the Levites: Men twenty-five years old or more shall come to take part in the work at the tent of meeting, but at the age of fifty, they must retire from their regular service *and work no longer. They may assist* their brothers in performing their duties at the tent of meeting, but *they themselves must not do the work.* This, then, is how you are to assign the responsibilities of the Levites."[2] (Numbers 8:23-26, emphasis added)

Levites could be called into service as young as twenty-five. David later added a five-year "internship" to this plan and included Levites as young as twenty. This part seems completely logical, exactly what you'd expect.

The part of the design most of us don't expect is that a Levite's service at the tent of meeting *stopped* at fifty.

But there's a catch.

Being fifty didn't signal the end of ministry. Older Levites weren't put out to pasture or forced into early retirement. Though they were actually no longer permitted to do this *particular* work, they could *assist*, serving as coaches, mentors, and cheerleaders (minus the pompoms) for younger generations.

The passage is explicit: "they themselves must not do the work."

Think about the impact those words could have on the church if we applied them even loosely today. Could this cryptic text hint at God's design for passing along leadership to the next generation? Could this design invite the over-fifty crowd to step out of leadership roles while they still have plenty of ability left so they can coach, assist, and develop the next generation from the sidelines?

Try throwing out this idea at an elders' meeting, and you might discover this kind of cheerleading really *is* the most dangerous sport in the church! Think about what might happen to your church if everyone over fifty suddenly stepped back from leadership. For most congregations, "dangerous" doesn't begin to describe the potential chaos.

On the other hand, what if, as a pastor, I knew from the very beginning of my ministry that at age fifty my leadership role would need to fundamentally shift, that I'd be stepping off the stage and moving into the wings? One thing's for sure: I'd give a lot more attention to developing leaders around me—a lot earlier—than most church leaders do now.

This provocative Bible passage shifts the lens of young adult ministry away from getting young adults to participate in the programs we design for them (sometimes for no greater purpose than getting them to come to more programs we design for them). The lens shifts to developing the next generation of leaders for God's people to take part in God's work.

Just how we make such a shift is the unapologetic focus of the rest of this book.

The End of the Conveyor Belt

Think about college graduation day for a moment. After a few pictures with family, graduates take their seats with all the other robed scholars in their flat hats, completing a journey begun in kindergarten.

After that last piece of cake, that last hug on a sweaty May afternoon, that last promise to keep in touch, the reality of adulthood comes crashing in. After twenty years of schooling, it's finally over. And life starts to get unsettlingly real.

For many young adults, this new life comes with its own brand of profound loneliness, making the years after college graduation, for some, the loneliest time in their lives. The built-in social circles of school are removed, and the conveyor belt of automatic community comes to an abrupt halt.

Stepping into this stage of life leaves many young adults unhinged and feeling more alone than they ever expected. Many look anywhere—online or otherwise—for places that might offer meaningful connections with *actual* people, places that provide purposeful outlets for their personality and gifts.

Young adults coming into our circles, into our ministries, and into our churches aren't just looking for a friendly place; they're looking for friends, for family. They aren't looking for a place that knows how to run effective social media campaigns; they're looking for a place to find and cultivate a new sphere of belonging and impact.

A young adult in his late twenties highlights this longing:

> My dad worked his butt off all the time. He grew up at the end of the Depression, and he knew what it was like to go without. He wanted to make sure my brothers and I never had to experience that, but we grew up instead without much of a relationship with him.
>
> I think many baby boomers grew up with a mentality that asked them to work very hard at giving *things*, but the children of baby boomers missed the *connection* with them altogether.

Here's a mixed bag of news:

* *Good news.* Most young adults highly value older generations and long to be connected with a resonant community that spans more than their own life stage.[3]
* *Bad news.* Only 16 percent of young adults regularly interact with any older mentors.[4]

Churches may wince at this reality, but we did it to ourselves. We've successfully socialized young adults into assuming that being in church primarily means being with people in their own life stage. Maybe that's why on-ramps to adulthood are so difficult to find.

How did this happen?

* We create a church nursery for babies.

* When babies get too old for the nursery, we create a children's church experience for them during worship.

* When children become teenagers, we create a high-energy middle school experience during worship.

* When kids finish eighth grade, we provide their own targeted high school worship service (to keep them from being bored in worship).

* Those who don't say goodbye to church when they say goodbye to youth group are shuffled off to a college and career group.

In many churches, it's become perfectly normal to spend one's entire childhood and adolescence without *ever* worshiping with people outside your age group, which reinforces the consumer culture that surrounds you every day. Because of an extensive focus on age-appropriate, attractional programs from birth through high school, many young adults who were highly active in their youth group were never truly part of their church.

They step into adulthood with a developmental and spiritual backdrop in which people of other generations have been almost completely absent from their faith development (apart from teachers and leaders running programs targeted to their specific needs).

No wonder the typical church's first response to this problem is to start another age-specific program, this time with the name "young adult" attached to it. In one church we visited, an older focus-group member suggested, "Easy. Just put them in a room with each other, add a guitar, and you're good to go!"

Instead of focusing on programs for young adults, let's start by focusing on building solid on-ramps to a multigenerational community for young adults. We don't do it because it's simply much more complex than creating and advertising a group that almost all young adults will ignore.

On-Ramps to Community

Not only do most churches not yet know how to build on-ramps to a multigenerational community, but most young adults don't know how to do it either. Indeed, they might not know how to get it or even how to articulate that they want it. But many young adults have a deep longing to connect with other generations. This is especially true for those who've spent their lives isolated from the rest of the church.

Take Jennifer, an active twenty-seven-year-old volunteer in her church. She grew up in a traditional, age-segregated program. But after finding a way into the life and leadership of her church, she described it this way:

> Being so engaged in the church has brought a sense of purpose in my life. I have a church where I am an important piece of the puzzle. Before, I only attended a service full of college students. We were all on the same path with the same goal. But now there are people from all walks of life, and their unique perspectives challenge me in so many ways.

When young adults do find an on-ramp for engaging with other generations, it can be a game changer for both generations. Believe it or not, these relationships, rather than the next greatest attractional gimmick, are what hold the greatest opportunity for sustained involvement in the life of your church.

As one author puts it:

If there's one lesson to take away from this corpus of literature [about young adults leaving the church], it's this: Intergenerational relationships are crucial. The number one predictive factor as to whether or not a young Christian will retain his or her faith is whether that person has a meaningful relationship with an older Christian.[5]

Researchers Allan Martin and Clint Jenkin echo this message: "For so many of our respondents, their relationship with the church was determined by their relationship with older members. These were even more important than peer relationships in many cases."[6]

When comparing young adults who stayed active in their faith after adolescence with those who dropped out of church, Barna's research confirms that those who stayed were almost *twice as likely* (59 percent versus 31 percent) to have a close personal friendship with an adult inside the church. Said another way, seven out of ten young adults who lost their connection with the church *did not* have a close relationship with an older adult.[7]

The fact is, when it comes to young adult ministry, intergenerational relationships serve as the glue for connection to church. But as statistics bear out, these kinds of relationships almost never happen on their own. They require intentional work.

This means you'll need to take a very practical step in building your church's young adult ministry: forming a "coaching squad."

Building Your Team

I have a friend who's a turnaround expert for high school football teams. He's now taken three teams with abysmal records to championships, each within three years or less. No matter what kind of talent pool he's handed (and almost always, as he says, "It ain't much"), his first priority, surprisingly enough, isn't to focus on the players but to assemble a coaching *team* to work his game plan. Any church that hopes to build a thriving young adult program needs to do the same thing.

Intergenerational impact begins by building your team of coaches. Watch for people whose eyes light up about the prospect of working on such ideas. You'll want at least three people on your team and no more than ten.

As you ask people to serve on this team, don't worry yet about handing them a job description. Starting out, the project is too open-ended for airtight roles. As you begin talking with possible coaches and cheerleaders in your church, you'll want to simply define the win, something like this:

> We want our church to be a place where young adults engage profoundly in God's mission. Some of them may stay for the rest of their lives, but most of them will be here for just a few years. We want our church to be the place where young adults have opportunity for service and relationship, and we want mentors who will help young adults make an impact for Christ in our community and our world. I'm not asking you to start a young adult Bible study or teach a Sunday school class. I'm asking you to partner with me and a few others for the next few years to create the kind of place that nurtures and develops the dreams of the next generation so profoundly that both the church and our young adults are changed in the process.

At this point, you'll certainly come across people who like *your* idea and are willing to *help*. You'll be tempted to put them on your coaching team.

Don't do it.

Let me say it again: some people will merely want to *help* you with *your* idea. Don't put them on your coaching squad.

You're looking for people who have as much (or more) passion as you do about this dream. One person on your team who's doing you a favor will diffuse the focus of the entire group. Helpers *eventually* will be great resources for you. But resist the temptation to put helpers on your coaching squad.

After recruiting your squad, it's time to pull them all together to clarify exactly what they're getting into. At your first meeting, start by having them each share why young adult ministry matters to them. Next, lay the groundwork, defining the process the team will be working. You can offer the sample ministry team job description (see "Ministry Job Descriptions" online) or draft your own based on the following basic template.

* *Invest in relationships.* Spend time with young adults, inviting them over for dinner and having coffee with them, all outside of structured programming.

* *Facilitate friendships.* Introduce young adults to people of other generations in the church.

* *Take the long view.* Be prepared to work this process with the team for at least three years.

* *Show up.* We don't yet know what venues will take center stage for our young adult ministry. If the venue is a food truck, this team will be regular customers. If it's a tutoring program, the coaches will be around. If it's a worship service, the coaches will be as regular as the furniture.

* *Provide guidance.* God told Moses that Levites older than fifty must not "do the work themselves" but must support the younger team. We'll offer wisdom and lend a hand when we can, but the young adults themselves will carry the weight of leadership.

* *Reciprocate.* Be willing to learn and receive from young adults, not just teach and give to them. Move beyond a transactional top-down relationship into a reciprocal, side-by-side relationship.

In this first gathering, you'll give the coaching squad the opportunity to update the covenant (job description) together and agree to a basic understanding of what they're committing to do. Once they've agreed to a covenant, provide a skeleton description of the process:

* We'll read this book together during the first three months.

* We'll continually develop a database of all the young adults we know who are in some way connected to our church.

* We'll meet with young adults one-on-one and in group settings until *their* vision of ministry in our community becomes clear, and then we'll figure out the next steps.

* We'll select a project (or projects) and work together to launch it (or them), side by side with young adults, who will take the lead, with our support.

* We'll expect that our first few prototype ideas won't work, so we'll be prepared to keep processing with our young adult friends, rebooting and trying new initiatives. We'll remember that no project is a failure if it provides an avenue to work alongside young adults and support them.

* We'll keep repeating the process of helping young adults live into their God-given missional dreams until we get the reputation for being *that place* in the community that really does help young adults move the needle.

There's a good chance your team will attempt to do things that haven't been done before, at least not at your church. Think of this work as a laboratory for the future church, its R & D department.

Of course, every laboratory has one thing in common—lots of failed experiments! But each failure can take your team one step closer to discovering just what you're looking for (usually *more* than you're looking for!).

Someone Has to Be the Head Coach

Our experience has been that any coaching squad won't make much progress without a head coach, a team leader. Many churches assume that the answer to their young adult problem will come in the form of a singular leader—a superhuman—who can be a one-person relational magnet for college students or twenty-somethings.

Too often ministries that take this approach end up riding a roller coaster of ups and downs, success and failure, all predicated on the comings and goings of these individual leaders. Though a point leader is crucial to any enterprise, the best kind of young adult ministry leader has more *spider* skills than *super* skills.

They are web-weaving connectors rather than stand-alone problem solvers. For some churches, the team leader might be a dedicated staff person. For many, it will be a dedicated volunteer.

You don't necessarily need a team leader who's the high-energy, upfront face of the young adult ministry. But you *do* need someone to keep the trains running on time (and, to extend the metaphor, to be ready to fix the trains, build new tracks, and dispatch work crews as needed). See "Ministry Job Descriptions" at ivpress.com /sustainable-young-adult-ministry for a sample job description for a team leader.

This person doesn't need to be the relational and spiritual center of the ministry but a leader-developer, the one who creates and maintains the platform for others (including young adults themselves) to exercise their gifts, who weaves the web of the ministry. Without this type of team leader in place, your ministry with young adults will likely sputter in fits and starts, typically unraveling before it gets off the ground.

Almost the Right Words

Finding a word to describe the young adult ministry role for this team of adults in your church has been tricky for me.

Though *cheerleading* is a great metaphor, it can give the impression that the job is to stay on the sidelines, out of the game. The word *coach* also can be interpreted as one who sits above young adults and gives them marching orders, advice, support, or systems analysis when things go wrong.

In a healthy, sustainable young adult ministry, the (sometimes only slightly) older adult leaders learn just as much from young adults as the young adults learn from them. By using the terms *coach* and *cheerleader*, a reciprocal partnership can easily be missed.

But ultimately, with fear and trembling about the potential confusion, I decided to stick with coaching language.

Here's why: the end goal of any coach is to see the *players* succeed, to have *them* win games. The goal of any coaching staff isn't to win the prize as the world's best coach but to win games. Your coaching team will consist of people looking for young adults to succeed and empowering *them* to have that kind of success.

The best way for young adults to learn how to lead the church in the future is for them to lead in the church now. And the best way for them to succeed in church leadership now is to be supported, coached, partnered with, and surrounded by a generation of cheerleaders, participating in the most dangerous sport in the church.

Paradox 4

*Reach One Young Adult at a Time
Through a System to Reach Them All*

> *Great things are not done by impulse, but by a series
> of small things brought together.*
>
> VINCENT VAN GOGH

> *Some "hard things" are actually "easy things"
> rebranded as impossible.*
>
> JEN HATMAKER

A few years ago, a couple came to me with a great idea to start an off-campus ministry for college students and young adults. They were passionate about their calling, and I couldn't help but be caught up in their enthusiasm about reaching the generation no one else seemed to be bringing into the life of the church.

As we talked over coffee, they painted the picture of what they imagined a group like this could look like. Clearly, they'd worked hard to cultivate the picture in great detail. They had a unique approach to large-group meetings and expressed concern that most young adult ministries settled for fifteen people or less. They were abundantly clear about the ways they wanted to engage young adults. I was impressed that they'd done their homework and knew what they were talking about.

The couple had a solid missional mindset and got it when it came to the intense relational needs of young adults. They'd already completed the necessary legal work to establish themselves as a nonprofit with an accompanying bank account. They had a name for this ministry and a vision for engaging hundreds, maybe even thousands, with their unique approach.

"How can I help?" I asked. They were seeking advice and, as I later learned, a space (one of our sites had a facility near campus with great meeting areas). In response, I shared some basic principles of this book.

The longer I talked, the more their faces fell. I described the year they'd need to prepare the soil for their launch and the infrastructure they'd need to build to support their dream. As I soon learned, this wasn't the kind of advice they were looking for.

They were ready to start today, and no one was going to stop them, least of all me.

Realizing I was losing them fast, I stopped and said, "There's a lot more we could talk about, but let's stop right there. Was any of that helpful?" They graciously affirmed my advice, hurriedly gathered their belongings, and headed out for their next meeting, promising to circle back in the near future. I never heard from them again.

They launched the ministry four weeks later, and I kept up with their social media posts and heard updates through mutual friends. After a year or so, participation in their weekly meetings settled at an average of around fifteen (with a high of twenty-five and a low of seven), almost all of them were already involved in their own churches.

When we finally reconnected, they said, "We love making such deep impact, transforming a few lives at a time."

Let me be clear: building a ministry to a group of seven to twenty-five young adults is nothing to be disappointed about. In fact, a group this size is an effective way to engage young adults. What this couple was achieving was important and valuable.

On the flip side, this couple had launched their ministry (and raised their funds) with a vision and expectation of reaching exponentially more. Pretending that a small-and-deep ministry was their original mission, they had reshaped the dream around the reality of the results that came through their hurry-to-launch approach.

So how did they fall so far short of their original dream?

I don't believe it was because they were bad leaders. They are great people who love God and ministry. I don't think it was because they weren't called; it seemed clear that God had a calling in their lives. I don't believe they had a bad idea. I think they had a unique approach with the potential to reach countless young adults disenfranchised from the church.

They had all the components, all the pieces needed to make this thing work, except for two very important things:

* They lacked the systems needed to support their dream.
* They lacked the patience to put those systems in place.

The Dance Floor

In his book *Sustainable Youth Ministry*, my coauthor, Mark, introduces a systems approach to ministry with a metaphor I find myself using frequently:

> Years of preparation had made her movements effortless, her turns seamless, her leaps weightless. A dancer of unparalleled talent, she mesmerized the crowd with her skill but even more with her passion. Her countenance

proclaimed in no uncertain terms that she was made for this moment.

But she would finish much sooner than anyone expected. Coming down from an arching leap, she landed with a jolting crack, her foot driving its way through the rotting wood of the floor, her body twisted in pain. . . . She was pulled from the stage, wondering if she would ever dance again.

The master of ceremonies dismissively apologized, "Inexperience does this to a dancer."

But no one came to repair the floor.

And then, as if nothing had happened, the next performer was introduced. The crowd responded with smattered applause. But with no one attending to the dance floor, the audience knew that the new dancer would also find her performance ending prematurely with a disappointing, perhaps tragic, conclusion.

"Attending to the dance floor" may be the most neglected task in [young adult] ministry. When the dance floor is not in place, talent is not enough. The right preparation is not enough. Not even passion and enthusiasm can prevent the inevitable dissatisfaction and disaster.[1]

This chapter introduces a "systems approach" to building a thriving young adult ministry. Throughout the rest of the book, I'll teach you the essential steps of building a solid dance floor for the work you're being called to do.

Biology Lesson

A system is simply a set of components and processes for getting something done. It includes a repetitive set of steps that connect each step to the whole in a way that produces a predictable result again and again.

All churches and all ministries have systems or ways things get done. Some have been intentionally built. Most have evolved over time, much like a meandering stream.

The tens of thousands of churches across America struggling with young adult ministry seldom actually have a young adult problem. They have a systems problem. Too many churches have unexamined systems in place that actually repel and predictably disengage young adults.

The church, like the human body, of course, isn't a single system. It's a system of systems. The body has the circulatory system, the digestive system, the respiratory system, the cardiovascular system, the nervous system. Depending on how you count them, the body has about twelve to fourteen different systems, all designed to work together so seamlessly that we hardly ever think about them. Systems in the church work (or don't) the same way.

To stretch the metaphor one step further, most young adult ministries get a nice femur, a lung, some veins, a large intestine, with skin thrown in for good measure. All these parts get together and wonder why in the world their body isn't working so well.

Many churches unintentionally assume that with just a few quality pieces they'll have a healthy congregation. Few ideas could be further from the truth, but those ideas are especially common in young adult ministry.

But This Is So Boring

When some friends built a new home near our neighborhood, we checked in with them every week or so about the progress. And because I drove by the building site every day on the way to work, I saw it regularly.

I remember our friends' early reports about the project, filled with excitement and anticipation. They were meeting with the architect, drawing up plans, working with the bank on the loan, going back and forth trying to nail down exactly what their dream house would look like. They'd walk the empty lot dreaming of the end result. They'd come "home" at different times of day to catch a glimpse of what their view would look like out the bedroom at sunrise, at midafternoon, at sunset. They had a friend take pictures of themselves digging the first shovelful of dirt for their home.

But after the digging started, the enthusiasm definitely started to wane. For weeks I'd drive by and see that almost nothing had changed. My friends began referring to their dream home as "the giant hole in the ground that we own."

In the meantime, the builders were spending their time grading the property, digging the hole just right, pouring and laying the layers of the foundation and basement. My friends checked in at the site regularly and always left a little sad. I wish I had a nickel for every time I heard them say, "It doesn't look much different from the last time we were here."

After weeks of this disappointing building journey, the walls started to go up and we began to see the outline of a home. Our friends could now walk through and imagine where the closets and bedrooms would go. We shared their excitement as they enthusiastically walked us through their framed house, announcing in painstaking detail where each closet and fixture would be.

Just when they thought they were actually moving the project forward, progress would slow again. The electrical wires had to be run through the house, new plumbing had to be added everywhere, and heating and cooling ducts had to be put in place. And once again, my friends wondered if any real progress was being made.

Building a young adult ministry—building it right, at least—will, at times, be boring, tedious, and disheartening. It's easy to grow impatient and want to take shortcuts.

Sadly, most churches would rather throw up some walls, tack on some siding, and call it good. They spend their time doing "the real work of ministry," in Bible study after Bible study, in coffee shop after coffee shop, and wonder why they're making so little difference. It's no surprise so many give up altogether.

Naming the Systems of Young Adult Ministry

Rather than dreaming up a catchy name or logo or coming up with the next great program idea, the church that wants to build a sustainable young adult ministry will start by knowing the essential systems a healthy, long-term ministry requires. Once those systems are in place and you've determined how to implement each one and in what order, then (and only then) are you ready to start leading the ministry you're building.

To make this topic more concrete, here are fifteen essential systems to put in place as you build a young adult ministry:

* The *volunteer system* provides a hernia-free process for recruiting, equipping, and dispatching volunteers into clearly defined roles that are life-giving for the volunteers and make an impact for the gospel aligned with the church's core values.

* The *visioning system* defines where the ministry wants to go and provides benchmarks for how it hopes to get there. Every single year it helps answer the questions: "Are we succeeding? Are we accomplishing what we believe God has called us to, what we set out to do?"

* The *discipleship system* identifies explicitly how a ministry's varied efforts work together to deepen and strengthen the faith of people involved.

* The *evangelism and mission system* defines the unique expression of the gospel that people involved in your ministry will bring to the surrounding community and the broader world, aligning their efforts for particular kingdom impact.

* The *compliance system* ensures that all legal requirements related to the ministry are met, including background checks, payroll filings, licenses, and so on.

* The *database system* allows us to stay appropriately connected so we don't communicate the same way with the long-term young adult member as we do with the twenty-year-old from Des Moines who attended an event three years ago.

* The *communication system* pulls together the multiple streams of communication into a coherent, strategic, integrated message that actually produces desired results. In today's noisy world, we need to hone the Goldilocks approach (not too much, not too little, but just right!).

* The *hospitality system* establishes clear processes to ensure that every person visiting our ministry experiences a surprisingly welcoming environment as well as consistent, noncreepy follow-up contacts.

* The *calendar system* ensures we aren't simply reacting to the most urgent demands but are also building a rhythm into the work we're called to do together. It also allows us to be strategic in how we expend our limited time, energy, and money on the highest leverage projects.

* The *regular programming system* establishes a steady drumbeat for delivering consistently well-executed programs that participants experience as well worth the time they invest.

* The *major event system* builds implementation teams that pull off effective, well-attended events, free of frustration, desperation, and volunteers who work at cross-purposes.

* The *innovation system* creates a space for developing initiatives that point your ministry toward its future, welcoming outside-the-box thinking from people without a long history in the organization.

* The *integration system* links together the various departments and ministry efforts to remove silos and ensure the healthy, appropriate integration of the generations and the varied strands of ministry.

* The *financial system* maximizes the generous investment of donors through faithful tracking and expenditure of funds, moving expressions of need, and meaningful expressions of gratitude.

* The *marketing/outreach system* implements deliberate strategies for engaging young adults not yet engaged in church life.

Yes, that's a lot of systems. And each system has many component parts.

But remember the human body. The skeletal system alone is made up of 206 *different* bones. And the muscular system has a whopping 600 *different* muscles.

Each ministry system has multiple component parts, all necessary to create sustainable ministry.

Lessons from Delta

In my experience, young adult ministries almost never fail because of the failure of a single component or two (e.g., "If we *just* had a great young adult leader," "If we *just* had a better worship experience," etc.). Almost always, failure predictably comes because of a fundamental lack of the systems required to ensure a thriving, sustainable ministry.

The fragmented, program-based approach almost never works. A systems approach, on the other hand, starts with the assumption that the ministry *requires* many interlocking pieces to work together.

So before you totally glaze over, assuming that systems work is about the least-exciting work you can imagine, I want to present a picture from the other side of the system.

My friend Andrea loves Delta Airlines. As someone who flies hundreds of thousands of miles a year, she long ago blasted past the platinum and diamond levels, all the way to the adamantium level. I sometimes wonder if she's accumulated enough miles to purchase the entire company!

At one point, Andrea had a family emergency. "I had to get my grandkids to my house right away," she says, "but there were many states and many thousands of miles between us."

So she called the Delta customer-service hotline—made for million-milers like her—explained her crisis, and asked for their help. Four hours later, her grandkids were at her door. Free of charge.

Aside from marveling at the out-of-this-world customer service Andrea experienced, I wondered, *What made this miracle happen?*

It didn't take me long to come up with the answer: *systems.*

Delta has a rewards program that Andrea has been part of for decades. The company knows her, knows her regular travel, knows the loyalty she's shown them over the years. Delta has a well-oiled database system to give them access to all the information they need at a moment's glance. Delta has a scheduling system that easily finds the closest airports with available seats. Even their customer-care system allowed Andrea to call right in and address an issue with someone who was empowered to make decisions on the spot.

Systems affect families. Systems affect people. Systems make a huge difference in the kind of impact any ministry can have. And so, though systems might feel like boring or even nonessential work, I'm guessing Andrea and her grandkids think otherwise.

You might have a dream to affect just one young adult. If that's your dream, I wish there were more of you in this world, but you don't need this book. You can start a relationship and follow where that trail leads by showing up consistently.

But if you are called to partner with others in your congregation or community to reach the largest, most unchurched generation in

America's history, you'll need to build a system that reaches twice or even three times the amount of young adults you think you'll reach personally. Only then, once the systems are working in concert, will we be able to do more than focus on one person at a time. We'll be able to repeat the process of reaching young adults again and again.

Paradox 5

*Respond to Lack of Commitment
by Asking for More*

> *The average age when formal leadership training starts is 42.
> We give leaders a 20- to 40-year head start.*
>
> KIDLEAD, EXECUTIVE LEADERSHIP TRAINING
> FOR AGES TWO TO TWENTY-FIVE

> *Joining my church's mission has brought a sense of purpose
> in my life. I have a church where I'm an important piece
> of the puzzle in making a difference.*
>
> CHELSEA, AGE TWENTY

With all I've already said about giving more responsibility to young adults, now might be a good time for a reality check. *Loyalty. Longevity. Responsibility. Follow-through.*

These probably aren't the *first* words you'd use to describe young adults. If you've done even cursory research on this generation, you're more likely to use *entitled, lazy,* and *unable to follow through on the simplest tasks.*

When it comes to planning ahead, Lauren, a college student, admits it's not a strong suit of her peers. She says,

> [Millennials] act as though social engagements, parties, and activities where people gather are more like opportunities. A smorgasbord of possibilities, if you will. They take in all the possible offers and then wait until the last minute to decide which one to attend based off of how beneficial it will be to them individually. It does not matter if they already agreed to go. If something better comes along, they'll go to that.[1]

Cassie, age twenty-seven, reflects a similar mentality: "I join about 12 Facebook events a month for shows or birthdays and go to something like two of them."[2]

And it's not just social engagements where young adults seem to lack staying power. Perceptions in the workplace are equally as incriminating:

* Seventy percent of all millennials will leave their first job within two years of starting.[3]

* Forty-five percent of companies experience high turnover with those employees identified as "millennials"—by a two-to-one margin versus older generations.[4]

In one poll, 68 percent of those surveyed say young adult employees are less motivated to take on responsibility and produce quality work than their counterparts in other age groups, and 46 percent believe young adults are less engaged at work than other employees.[5]

If we approach our young adult ministry with those same assumptions about young adults, we'll likely move in exactly the wrong direction. We'll assume the only way to work with young adults is to expect little of them, knowing that so few actually stick around once their initial interest fades.

And that approach would be a huge mistake, one I'm sure Karen is glad her church didn't make with her.

Today, Karen is a supervolunteer in her church's youth ministry. But it didn't start out that way. She was typically late or absent for team meetings, regularly texting at the last minute about why she'd have to miss. She cited excuses such as a full class schedule, too much homework, or just "life." Karen was stretched to the limit and didn't really have space for youth ministry.

She didn't have space until she was approached a different way. Instead of lowering the bar and asking Karen to take on even less than her current one-hour-a-week volunteer role, the youth pastor invited her to make a deeper commitment: *run* the winter retreat.

Although this was an exponentially greater commitment, more like ten hours per week for a month or two, something clicked.

Maybe it was because this opportunity gave Karen something to direct and own rather than just help out. Maybe it was because this was a seasonal commitment rather than an open-ended weekly one. Maybe this challenge tapped into her organizational genius.

Regardless, Karen's story provides a great picture of the young adult mindset. It's not that they don't have time or ability to follow through on commitments. Like Karen, most young adults make time for what matters to them. Despite the stereotypes of laziness and inconsistency, young adults desire to make an impact, and if an opportunity taps into that desire, their likelihood of staying committed and interested shoots way up. They desire deeper commitments, even though they have trouble making them.

The Relative Value of Time

A friend with more than a decade of ministry experience (who now serves as a consultant for other churches) recently described her disappointing experience *trying* to volunteer at her home church. She told the youth director that her travel schedule (due to coaching other youth ministries) made her unavailable most Sundays but that she'd love to help with the midweek youth group or maybe a small group during the week.

The youth director seemed pleased and said he'd find something to fit this eager volunteer's schedule. A week later, he called back and asked if she'd take responsibility for updating the youth ministry bulletin board once a month.

My friend was understandably disappointed—and not because the job was too hard. She certainly could have done the bulletin board in *much less* time than she was planning to volunteer to actually work with students. But the offer felt like a massive misappropriation of her gifts.

Even she was curious about her gut-level reaction: "It's funny. Ask me to change your bulletin board once a month—maybe a thirty-minute job—and I don't have time. But ask me to do something that takes several hours a week but fits my gifts—like overhauling the struggling junior high program or launching a new group for middle school girls—and I'll find the time!"

Churches everywhere struggle with the lack of commitment they see in young adults. They seem to show up for a season, promise a lot, and then disappear. A young adult once committed to take a key role in our ministry and enter into our internship program only to drop out less than a month later.

The key is understanding that time is a relative concept in the young adult universe. On the surface, they may seem overscheduled, with way too much on their plates. It's easy to assume this population won't have time for the church. But ask them to join a mission that resonates with their own gifts and—bam!—they suddenly have time. Research backs it up.

* In 2014, almost a quarter of young adults volunteered forty or more hours for causes they cared about.

* Seventy-seven percent of young adults said they're more likely to volunteer when they can use their specific skills or expertise to benefit a cause.[6]

With seemingly unavailable young adults, the best approach may seem to be lowering the bar and asking less of them. What if the best solution is actually asking *more*, inviting them to greater levels of ownership and leadership in the church? Certainly this won't work for everybody, but for some it will serve as the gateway into fruitful, profound engagement.

It sure worked this way for Erin, a twenty-something in our church, but not without first creating a little discomfort for me.

As the church's worship coordinator, Erin spent three to five hours a week organizing our worship teams. When we met for lunch, she was amped—brimming with big ideas. I assumed this lunch was about ideas she had for the worship team but couldn't have been more off. She had ideas for how the *entire* church might engage in mission more faithfully together.

While Erin talked, I realized I'd been seeing her only in the category of worship coordinator. And honestly, she fit well into that slot. But she made it clear she had much more to offer than I gave her credit for.

And offer she did. As our dreaming and brainstorming came to a close, Erin said, "This is the reason I'm here. This is the reason I want to be part of this church. Can I go for it?"

As the pastor, I had a decision to make. I could keep things tidy and confine Erin to the slot where she was serving ("Just play your position, and let me worry about the big picture"). Or I could give her permission to step out, knowing that her ideas weren't part of any linear strategic plan the church or I had developed. What if, I wondered, creating a laboratory for innovation—a place for young adults to make their creative contributions—became *part* of our linear strategy?

I decided if I was serious about engaging young adults, not just getting them to show up, I'd need to make room to see them in new ways, viewing their desire to make an impact as intimately tied to our call as the church. I had to recognize that Erin's ideas weren't simply from a single, enthusiastic young adult. They were an expression of the unanswered cry of a generation: "Help me make an impact!"

I couldn't help but hear the implied message: "And if I can't make an impact here, I'm not going to wait. I'll make an impact somewhere else."

The End of Assimilation: A Modest Proposal

In the last decade or so, how we've thought about and involved young leaders in decision-making has drastically changed (and it needed to).

It used to be a normal, effective practice for key leaders to sit around the decision-making table and then report their decisions to younger apprentices. Young leaders took their cues from the older decision-makers and implemented those people's decisions.

Some younger leaders expressed a desire for a voice in the process, but more simply left the church. Many young leaders assumed (often correctly) they could make a more profound contribution through a nonprofit startup or through their secular employment than by waiting for the older generation to allow them a meaningful seat at the decision-making table.

Today, younger leaders have gone a step further, desiring not just a voice but an actual opportunity to shape decisions. Today, the only way to truly work with younger leaders is to make sure their voice and their values affect the outcome.

I'm a systems guy; that much has been clear throughout the book, I hope. I've spent lots of time trying to understand how to build systems that ensure a healthy, grounded culture in churches. Healthy churches don't make up processes as they go. They read books, attend seminars, and avoid reinventing the wheel as much as possible.

In many churches, the assimilation system has been popular for decades. It's designed to help move people to deeper involvement at church, from being guests and visitors to contributing members.

I've come to believe that *assimilation* is a terrible word for what we're trying to do with young adults. It conjures up images of a *Star Trek*-themed clone-making assembly line. Assimilation assumes that the most important questions churches should ask about new members are, "How do we transition them into the dominant culture of our church? How do we get them to buy into what we've created and support it with their time and money?"

It's time to give up trying to assimilate the next generation. That ship has sailed. We might find ourselves lowering the commitment bar just to get them to jump over it and join what we're doing, but young adults aren't interested in being absorbed into the dominant culture of our churches. They want a role in shaping and creating an entirely new culture.

Here's my modest proposal: find ways to deliberately share the responsibility for shaping your church's future with the generation you'd like to see lead it in the next fifteen to twenty years. Consider creating a Next Generation Leadership Academy.

Here's the basic idea: most churches have little if any process in place for cultivating a new generation of leaders. The best that most can imagine is trying to include a token young person (read: under forty) to serve on the leadership board. In our observation, these experiences are often exercises in frustration, with young voices routinely stifled by the status quo and an old guard annoyed by new ideas from upstart young leaders.

What if a Next Generation Leadership Academy became a normal part of the workings of every church? It could happen naturally—when the only churches left in twenty years are those that have successfully found ways to engage the coming generation's leadership power.

Though the details can vary, a Next Generation Leadership Academy contains the following components.

* A cohort of young adults deliberately engaged in a higher commitment group to empower them with the foundations of leadership: spiritual, financial, vocational, ministry, missions, administration, compassion, teaching, and so forth.

* A venue for this group to provide evaluative and innovative input on every area of church life.

* Reciprocal mentoring relationships in which members of younger and older generations learn from one another.

* An apprenticeship rotation (similar to a medical residency) in which every young leader apprentices in the church's key ministry areas (worship, missions, youth, etc.).

* Regularly scheduled pastoral listening sessions, where young leaders tell the pastor anything they're seeing or hearing—in the church or the world—that the church needs to pay attention to.

The goal is to make it normal to have space for young leaders not to be assimilated into the church's dominant culture but to become co-creators of it.

Like every initiative with young adults, though, we anticipate that building a Next Generation Leadership Academy requires a commitment to a multiyear process of beta testing, prototyping, evaluating, and improving. For a more detailed proposal for a Next Generation Leadership Academy go to ivpress.com /sustainable-young-adult-ministry.

A Working Prototype

Chris Sasser, a friend and fellow Ministry Architects consultant, found a way to develop the leadership capacity of young adults when he launched the Leadership Journey. He was looking for a new way—beyond the typical approach of drawing young adults into church programming—of doing young adult ministry at his church in Wilmington, North Carolina.

So instead of returning to what he knew wouldn't gain much traction or have much impact, Chris focused on equipping young adults for changing the world with the gospel. Soon he realized the cards had been stacked in his favor. He says,

> We had college students graduating who wanted to make an impact. But they felt like their options were limited. They couldn't afford to do a "clean water for Africa" trip, and they weren't looking to give up their jobs and go on Young Life staff. Some of them were doing a gap year after college to focus on mission but only a small fraction.

So Chris started by creating an equipping ministry specifically designed for juniors and seniors in college. He sets the admission cost high. Every member fills out an application and, if selected, commits to an in-depth leadership-development program. The Journey meets once a week during the academic year and includes weekly training in some aspect of Christian leadership, small-group accountability, a mission initiative, and even homework.

For the first few weeks, the focus is on discernment, as group members seek to discover ways they're each uniquely wired for ministry. The rest of the first semester grounds them in the biblical narrative of leadership.

In the second semester, young people are introduced to a few key leadership books and to faithful, effective leaders from the community. Each student meets weekly throughout the length of the program with an older adult coach. In the process of doing life together, the coach works to integrate the concepts being learned with the craft of leadership, all while being attentive to the ways and places God is at work.

A natural byproduct of the Leadership Journey is authentic community. The fact that it's a byproduct and not the goal is a subtle but important distinction. Chris didn't set out to create a young adult *fellowship* that would attract people, but community happened through being in the trenches together. In fact, community happened in much more profound ways than it might ever have happened in a group designed specifically *for* fellowship.

Most participants begin not knowing many other group members. But the *third space* of shared mission ends up creating such a transforming power that a rich sense of community is unavoidable. The Journey process has had such a profound impact on students that most find themselves signing up for a second year that has more extensive requirements.

Chris has capitalized on the in-between season of young adulthood, providing a high-demand, high-commitment experiment in Christian leadership. After completing the first year, more than one participant has described the experience as their single most important faith step.

Chris isn't focused on attracting young adults with a low-threshold, easy-commitment program. This demanding training program offers young adults an intensive, résumé-building internship in project management, ministry, and mission. And the high commitment on the front end raises the stakes and signals that this is anything but "youth group 2.0."

No Easy Button

Let that story give you hope. You don't need show-stopping, hip programming (like those one or two churches in your town have) for a profound ministry with young adults. Hopefully, you begin to see that a ministry such as the Leadership Journey might work in your congregation, even with a handful of young adults you currently know.

But before rushing to launch your own equipping ministry for young leaders in your church and community, you'll want to count the cost. Scale your vision to what your church can afford, not so much in dollars but in *time* you'll need to invest. Counting the cost can be painful, but not nearly as painful as skipping this step. For us, it was agonizing.

Our church was recently on the receiving end of a wonderful opportunity. We were offered access to a prime piece of real estate in the hub of a housing development right next to a university. The space included offices, a large gathering space, a café, and a media room—it was amazing!

The best part? More than a thousand students live within walking distance. The property developers were interested in a Christian organization investing in the students living there. All we had to do was move in and initiate some kind of ministry. As our church leaders and I toured the space, our minds raced with ideas:

* "All we have to do is hire a part-time college student to run this thing."
* "If we just put a band in here on a Sunday morning, we'll have a new church in a month!"
* "With some great marketing, this place will fill up with college students."

In those first euphoric moments, our ideas for maximizing this opportunity flowed easily. We'd found "the easy button"—until we looked more closely.

As we dug into the complexity of this arrangement and our available resources, we couldn't see a way to make this opportunity work for the long haul. We didn't have a leader with the margin to invest. We didn't have the finances to even launch a ministry, much less handle the ongoing maintenance and overhead of a new space. Certainly, we could have *just done something* in that space, but the opportunity, the need, and our available resources didn't match up.

Although it broke our hearts to let this pass by, we knew the "we *just* need to" solutions we imagined on our first visit would have resulted in underplanning, understaffing, underresourcing and, as a result, underperforming and underachieving our vision for ministry.

With disappointing regularity, churches approach young adult ministry with an easy-button mentality, throwing a few spare dollars or an inexperienced leader in the general direction of young adults, hoping to get them to show up and engage even once. An opportunity presents itself and we dive in without a fully developed, adequately resourced, sustainable game plan, and unsurprisingly it doesn't work out.

Young adults function within a paradox of time that's different from what we might assume. Just because they don't have time to *attend* doesn't mean they don't have time to lead, create, or build. For the church to capture the imagination and potential of the next generation, it takes a commitment to embrace this paradox and raise the bar for young adults within the church. Not just the bar of expectations but also the bar of responsibility, accountability, and leadership.

That kind of approach can't start with "just doing something." It takes careful planning and courageous implementation of a new way of reaching and equipping young adults. The shortcut, easy-button approach seems so much simpler. But it can't hold a candle to the slow, deliberate cultivation process required for the kind of young adult ministry you've been praying for.

Paradox 6

*Attract Young Adults to Your Church
by Sending Them Away*

> *Indecision is a key characteristic of young adulthood.
> But then again, maybe not.*
>
> SAMANTHA HENIG AND ROBIN MARANTZ HENIG

> *You can't really ask them to live and breathe the company.
> Because they're living and breathing themselves
> and that keeps them very busy.*
>
> MARIAN SALZMAN, PRESIDENT OF EURO RSCG
> WORLDWIDE PR NORTH AMERICA

A few years ago, our worship band had become a tight-knit group. The members worked tirelessly on their craft, wrote songs, entered music festivals, and even recorded an album. They dreamed of using their talents in wider circles and made extensive plans about what that might look like. They wanted to make an impact.

Just as the dream was beginning to materialize, one band member landed a full-time job teaching music in another state. Another left for a position in another church. Another pursued missions in Africa. Before long, we had a band of rotating musicians, doing a fine job but definitely not living the original band's dream.

You know what we call this phenomenon in young adult ministry? Normal. Absolutely normal.

It's a rare young adult who puts down roots, works on a project past the promising beginnings, through the messy middle, and all the way through to completion, even if it was *their* dream in the first place!

There's no tragedy in this reality; it's normal. What *is* tragic, though, are the ways this normal reality totally stymies most churches in their work with young adults. Our churches are, by and large, structured to assimilate people who are geographically and vocationally stable. So we find ourselves focusing our young adult ministry on a tiny slice of the young adult demographic pie.

It's time to embrace the reality that most young adults are much too transient to fit into our tidy ministry systems, built on an assumption of permanence that's no longer even close to reality.

Take Jasmine Wanek, for example. In 2013, *USA Today* introduced the twenty-six-year-old conservation biologist from Baltimore as a prototypical young adult:

> [Jasmine] lost her parents a few years ago, then watched as their Forest Hill, Md., home, north of the city, sat on the market for a year with no buyers. Her Realtor even suggested at one point that they throw in one of the family's vehicles, a 1999 Isuzu Rodeo, to sweeten the deal. Wanek took the house off the market last spring. Then, after putting it up for sale again a few weeks ago, she got three offers, one of which she accepted. Closing day is November 15.
>
> She's moving to Daytona Beach, Fla., to move in with her fiancé, a flight attendant for Southwest Airlines. They'll

probably move again in a few months—he has a tiny, one-bedroom apartment a few minutes from the beach, and she's looking for a job down there.

Meanwhile, Wanek is working to settle her parents' estate—she posted a Craigslist ad offering their "barely used" Toro snow blower for $150. She's also trying to figure out how to get two pets—Harley, her 15-year-old West Highland terrier, and Tomato, her 7-year-old red-footed tortoise—down to Florida with her.

"Surprisingly, the dog and the tortoise are making things more complicated," she said. Wanek grew up in suburban Harford County, attended the University of Maryland and still has many friends here, but said, "I didn't want to stay in one place my whole life. . . . This is a good time for me to check out something else."[1]

What's the possibility that your young adult ministry could ever get on Jasmine's radar when she moves to your town?

A recent US Census Bureau statistic reveals that a whopping 30 percent of Americans in their twenties will move at least once *this year*, more than double the rest of the population.[2] And according to a Future Workplace survey, more than 90 percent of young adults *expect* to stay at their current job for less than three years.[3]

Although transience and mobility are a fundamental fact of life for young adults, churches tend to build programs around the mythical young adults who

* will be around for a while and can be mentored into long-term leadership.

* are interested in an exclusive relationship with our church and aren't church hoppers.

* are so grateful for our church that they'd never want to see it change.

* understand that they are *future* leaders and should be prepared to pay their dues for a decade or more before being given real leadership.
* will get married, stay around, and have children who grow up in our church.

Reggie McNeal, in *The Present Future*, describes a very different kind of young adult:

> Increasingly we are finding people who "belong" to two or more churches. A young man on a plane recently recounted to me his involvement with four churches that he considered himself a part of (one for worship, one for mission trips, another for their teaching ministry, and a fourth for their need of his technical expertise). The reason church leaders don't understand this growing trend is the institutional implications: We don't know how to count this participation or take up the offering in this new kind of world.[4]

For young adults, transience, mobility, and keeping options open are essential ingredients to the recipe for the good life. It's time to stop building ministries for a kind of young adult who no longer exists.

Working with the Grain

What if churches choose to work *with*—not against—the grain of who young adults are amid transition? What if we stop trying to build young adult ministries on the same kind of foundation we have built ministries to the far-less-transient populations of children, youth, and older adults?

It's easy for church leaders to complain about the young adult penchant for transience, for always keeping their options open. The words of one pastor echo the sentiments of hundreds of others: "Transient people often have a consumer attitude toward church.

They attend one church as long as it meets their needs better than another. You don't know who you can count on. People are fickle and tend to be critical. Rather than saying, 'We're part of this and we're going to make it go,' they act as if the church is on probation."[5]

At one level, of course, this pastor is absolutely right. But I wonder if he isn't missing some of the fundamental advantage that comes with working with a generation "on the move," a generation untethered. Consider the opportunities:

* Young adults' mobility and thirst for novelty make them prime candidates to plug in quickly to mission opportunities, both locally and globally.

* The passion to make an impact and do meaningful work provides the church with ready resources for mission. The explosion of programs such as Teach for America and AmeriCorps shows that this generation is ripe to be engaged in meaningful work, even if it means not making much money for a while.

* Young adults' absolute commitment not to waste their time on activities that aren't meaningful to them challenges churches toward greater excellence and faithfulness.

* Because of their hunger for mentors and eagerness to make meaningful contributions, many who might not otherwise darken your church's door could be open to participating in a program that equips them and allows them to impact the community and world.

* Even young adults who don't claim the Christian faith may be eager to participate in a community-impact opportunity sponsored by your church, providing an unparalleled opportunity for building new relationships.

* Although many people in the church are inherently resistant to change and innovation, young adults welcome and thrive on it.

If we hope to seize the opportunity presented by this "untethered generation," we'll want to consider ministry for and with them in radically different ways, ways that challenge our traditional template.

Could the mobility and transience of young adults offer an unmatched opportunity for ministry?

Key Shifts Required for Reaching a Generation Untethered

If you're convinced and want to switch to a ministry approach that takes seriously the transient reality of young adults, I propose six strategic shifts you'll need to make:

1. Shift from speaking to the group to speaking to the one. If you're part of an average church, you rely heavily on traditional forms of church advertising—bulletin announcements, bulletin boards, video announcements, Facebook posts, maybe even group texts or emails. These methods can create visibility for young adult ministry but will never be enough to actually get one off the ground.

This approach to promotion and engagement is based on the underlying assumption that everyone is simply waiting around for something (else) to engage them—spiritually or otherwise—and all we need to do is invite them in an interesting way, and they'll show up.

Young adults (and increasingly the rest of the population) simply don't live that way. With the average American bombarded by an estimated three thousand advertising messages a day, most have learned to survive the onslaught by expertly filtering out almost every advertisement in their lives, especially if the next step is somewhat complicated or requires lots of initiative.[6]

Some young adults are actually surprised to find a church that connects with them beyond blanket advertising. I saw it clearly on a recent Sunday morning.

I had a conversation with twenty-something sisters visiting our church with their significant others. We chatted for a few minutes after the service and then said goodbye.

The sisters' mom, a member of our church, caught me the next day and said—to my amazement—what an "incredible impact" our conversation had on her daughters. "It's all they talked about over lunch," she told me.

I replayed the conversation in my head and, for the life of me, had no idea what she was talking about. She must have seen my confusion, so she explained: "They've never really connected in a church before and are both on the verge of disconnecting from faith altogether. They were so surprised that someone would take a genuine interest in them personally. Church is usually a place where they come, listen, and leave. They finally felt connected."

We'll never engage a significant number of young adults in church life by relying on shotgun communication. (I'm including those ever-so-convenient, impersonal group emails and texts.) Especially at the beginning, one-on-one communication is always our best bet for building a group from the ground up.

Sure, there will be time for group communication *after* the group has coalesced or when people need reminders of commitments. But until then, talk to the one, not just the group.

2. Shift from stadium events to small cohorts. For years, the church has bought into the mentality that "bigger is (always) better." And though we certainly want to engage as many young adults as possible, their transient, often-disconnected culture precludes the likelihood of launching a young adult ministry with a model that begins with large, attractional events.

We can easily shrink the scale by focusing on creating smaller shared experiences. In a room designed for a thousand, one hundred young adults will wonder, *Where is everyone?* But when you meet two people for coffee and four show up, it feels as if *lots* of people are investing in this project.

Shrinking the scale allows us to create meetings that always feel full, based on the context we create. When you set up the meeting with an email saying, "I'm having a few people over to . . ." you're able to set expectations for something other than a huge gathering.

Young adults have plenty of options for large gatherings, and they're certainly drawn to big events. But to help them actually connect and find a place that feels like home, they need people who know them. Young adults will find far more reason to stick around when they're engaged with friends than when they're entertained in a crowd. Find a way to scale down by drawing smaller cohorts of young adults together, and you'll find stronger connections and deeper impact.

3. Shift from brilliant messages to transformational environments. Young adults thrive in self-directed learning environments. They've learned to follow up on their questions immediately and find new information on their own at warp speed. It's not surprising that so many of them have a hard time with traditional, presentation-style church programs.

If you have doubts, try this experiment: ask a group of young adults to spend an hour with you without access to their smartphones, tablets, and laptops. If you can get them to agree, pay attention to how often they instinctively reach for a device to look up some information as the conversation rolls along.

Who was the actor in that movie we're talking about? What was the score of last night's game? What is the distance between the earth and the sun? As a reflex, young adults have grown accustomed to having all the information they need at their fingertips. They've been socialized into learning interactively and finding ways to interact even when someone up-front is presenting information.

By contrast, many pastors have been taught to spend an hour of preparation for every minute of preaching. By this rule of thumb, the average pastor writing a twenty-minute sermon should spend roughly half the workweek preparing excellent messages for the congregation!

Though this strategy may have worked in generations past (though I wonder), it definitely won't build an effective young adult ministry. The best "sermons" might take place at Starbucks, over email, on a blog, or in settings in which no clear teacher is giving "right answers."

Rather than spending disproportionate hours on our presentations, we can create environments where transformational learning takes place. In a cohort or community marked by the authenticity of sharing doubts, failures, and hunches, we can begin looking at the right questions, the kind that will connect deeply with the faith of young adults today. We can listen and point to the ways that faith (and its unsettling sister, doubt) becomes real.

4. Shift from long-term contracts to short-term intensity. Even cell phone companies are getting the message. More and more are offering no-contract plans. Marketers are learning they may have a better chance of earning loyalty by *not* locking customers in (can you hear the prison doors clang?). Ironically, customers may be *more likely* to stay with a cell phone provider when they *aren't* expected to make a long-term commitment.

This approach flies in the face of the membership model most churches have been built on—a model that doesn't make sense to the average young adult. Especially at the beginning of your ministry launch, think in terms of shorter, more intense opportunities rather than plans dependent on long-term commitment. A weekend retreat or Saturday morning service project followed by lunch out has a much better chance of helping move a young adult ministry forward than launching a sixteen-week discipleship class.

One-off experiences with a reunion four weeks later give the potential for longer-term engagement without a requirement of commitment on the front end. Young adults are also much more likely to invite their peers to a single event than to an established group that's been meeting weekly for years.

5. Shift from depth to challenge. Pope Francis is a great example of a church leader gaining the admiration of young adults. Chosen in a conclave in 2013 after the unusual resignation of Pope Benedict XVI, Pope Francis immediately began making waves by modeling his faith with more than just words.

Sometimes referred to as Pope Francis the Revolutionary, this iconic leader of the Catholic Church has rejected fancy robes in exchange for modest attire. He has stooped low to wash the feet of female prisoners and transformed the mansion of a German bishop into a soup kitchen.

In his first papal exhortation, Pope Francis wrote, "I prefer a church which is bruised, hurting, and dirty because it has been out on the streets, rather than a church which is unhealthy from being confined and from clinging to its own security."[7]

Young adults can sense when a church is mired in routine and tradition so long that it no longer offers a challenge to the wider culture of the church and world. Though this generalization may not apply to every young adult, they tend to be less interested in deep intellectual and theological conversations and more awakened by a spiritual challenge to be lived out in the real world.

Though conflicting statistics abound regarding how few Christian young adults actually exist, it's fascinating what *kind* of Christians they are. It's not surprising that in the late 2000s and early 2010s, Shane Claiborne's book *The Irresistible Revolution*, David Platt's book *Radical*, and Francis Chan's book *Crazy Love* were top sellers for this generation of Christians.[8] They all offer an unapologetic call for Christians to give everything they have for the sake of the cross and reflect a young adult desire to be challenged in their faith.

6. *Shift from gathering to sending.* We often think evangelism and discipleship have different goals: one attracts outsiders to the truth of God, and the other gathers followers of Jesus around his transformational power so they become more like him. Step 1: Draw them here. Step 2: Anchor them here.

For many in the church, discipleship has been about meeting for the purpose of engendering long-term stability and spiritual growth. But the transience of young adults is forcing us to understand that discipleship may come just as profoundly (maybe even more so) through *sending* as through gathering.

In the first-century church, being a disciple and being sent out with the gospel were one and the same, not two different things. Disciples grew in their faith as they were sent beyond Jerusalem. Paul lived out his discipleship in missionary journeys. Although it's certainly possible to do faithful discipleship with a gathering-focused approach, it may be time to reclaim sending as a key discipleship strategy.

Because we know most young adults won't stay in one place for long, we can focus on preparing young adults for the next stage of their journeys, which—for most—won't include our particular church. We can spend the short time we might have with them aware that it is likely they will—sooner or later—leave for another faith community.

In my youth ministry days I ran a student leadership program for high school juniors and seniors. At that time, many youth pastors—myself included—viewed student leadership as the core of our *existing programs*. Student leaders became the primary influencers and inviters of friends and underclassmen, providing us with invaluable input about retreats, programs, and events.

But a mentor gave me a different perspective: "The main thing in student leadership is to prepare them to be another church's best volunteers. I want them each to be able to walk into a church in their first year of college and become an effective leader in that ministry, not simply helping our ministry be more successful."

The same lesson can be applied when it comes to young adult ministry. This is expressed clearly by a wise pastor:

> Now I view departures from a broader perspective. Our church is able to have an impact on people across the country and world. Three of our members are in Saudi Arabia right now, leading small groups. Whatever we give people that is good, right, and helpful—introduce them to a new ministry tool, give them a solid, biblical philosophy of ministry—they will take it away from here and multiply it elsewhere. So it's not a total loss. In one sense we're privileged. We've become a sending church.[9]

Reframing ROI

Somewhere along the line I'm sure I'll hear from readers: "We're just not getting the return on our investment that we were hoping for." Most of us hope to have a ministry that ends up filling *our* churches with spiritually alive young adults. And we assume the best way to get there is to get them here and keep them here.

Because the reality is more complex, let me share an old parable from *The Edge of Adventure* by Keith Miller and Bruce Larson:

> A note was found in the desert beside an old rusty water pump that said,
>
> Dear Friend,
>
> This pump is all right. . . . I put a new sucker washer in it and it should last for at least five years. But the washer dries

out and the pump has to be primed. So under the white rock to the north I've buried a bottle of water out of the sun and corked it up.

There's enough water in the bottle to prime the pump, but not if you take a drink first. Pour about one-fourth of the water and let it soak the leather washer. Then pour in the rest medium fast and pump like crazy. You'll get water.

This well has never run dry. Have some faith. Then, when you've pumped all the water you need, fill the bottle and put it back where you found it for the next feller who travels this path.

—Desert Pete[10]

I want to make the audacious claim that your best hope of having a church flowing with young adults is to risk being a church focused on sending them away from your church. It's time to stop working against the untethered tendency of college students and twenty-somethings and instead find ways to embrace and work with it.

If this kind of paradox feels familiar, it's because you've heard it from Jesus—and seen it in his life. God's economy works differently from ours. We can redefine the notion of a "sending ministry" as a "flowing ministry." Sending isn't losing; it's creating a space for young adults to flow through our churches in ways that are life-giving for them and for us.

Churches that have the courage to change their assumptions, to build a ministry geared toward adults who will be around only for a little while, will find that the impact on their own congregation (not to mention the larger church) might be more profound and vital than it ever could've been using the old model.

You might find exactly what you're hoping for—just not in the way you thought.

I Don't Know . . . Yet

Practicing the Long Obedience

> *One of the great disadvantages of hurry*
> *is that it takes such a long time.*
>
> G. K. CHESTERTON

> *You can have it all. Just not all at once.*
>
> OPRAH WINFREY

I 'll be honest: writing this book has been a challenge. At first I thought it would be a great way to get my ideas out in the world. I thought it was a way to respond to all the young adult ministry blogs without having to visit *every* comment section. And, if I'm honest, I thought it might be a way to make me feel smart.

But it didn't.

It made me feel dumb.

I started this project feeling like an expert in young adult ministry. After all, I had already implemented ideas and had extensive experience in the field. Then my coauthor, Mark, started asking me questions, an endless series of annoying "how will this help the ordinary church" questions.

And more often than I care to admit, I didn't know the answer—at least not yet. Mark would say, "Right now, we have ideas. What we don't have is a proven process that actually *works*." And he was right.

Fortunately, I had a laboratory provided by my consulting work through Ministry Architects. Each church I worked with gave me the chance to beta test, prototype, and iterate. With each new iteration, I approached my work like a research scientist, searching for the right alchemy for each new context.

During the four years it took to write this book, I closed the young adult church I was leading, and self-doubt haunted me. I've wondered at times whether my ideas might work only in my own head. But four years is a lot of time to observe the realities of real-life churches.

One was First United Presbyterian Church in Belleville, Illinois. On my visit there, I spent a day with group after group listening to their dreams and struggles in young adult ministry. The pastor had brought me in to do an assessment and to provide a working plan for moving forward.

To make the experience more interesting, my schedule leading up to the trip was jam-packed, my kids were ornery at my departure, and I faced major travel issues getting there. But once I arrived at the church, I was inspired by a surprising pattern. Every listening group shared the almost exact same story—a story that reminded me why this project matters so much.

This remarkably healthy congregation was doing fine, despite having little-to-no young adult ministry. By the time of my visit, they'd gone so far as to recruit a team leader and a young adult ministry team to begin thinking about reaching students at the small college down the street.

In focus group after focus group I heard this surprising perspective: "We don't even care if they come to church here. This is an underserved age group we need to care about."

And over and over, church members affirmed, "We have absolutely no idea what to do next."

The more I listened, the more it became abundantly clear: they were desperate for a plan. They had resources to invest. They had people to lead. The whole church was committed.

The light bulb clicked on, and I began to see how acutely lost churches can feel when it comes to ministry with young adults. I realized there are few if any accurate road maps to help churches take the right next steps.

If I could've read these chapters aloud to the saints at First United, they would've gobbled them up. They would've nodded in agreement about the six mistakes (I can imagine them saying, "Oh, so that's why . . ."). They would've been eager to implement the principles of the paradoxes as well as the sample implementation plan in this chapter.

They were ready to *do something*, but they had no idea what to do or how to do it. And they aren't alone. The vast majority of churches want to do *something* to reach young adults, but almost all of them are stuck. They simply don't know what to do next.

As one woman in Belleville said, "Everyone's always talking about how young adults are turned off by the church. What if we're the reason they choose to stay away for good?" Some churches become paralyzed and wonder, "What if we're *that* church?" No wonder some congregations never reach the starting line with young adults.

If you've wondered throughout this book exactly what to do next, this chapter is for you.

I Don't Know . . . Yet

Friedrich Nietzsche said, "The essential thing 'in heaven and earth' is that there should be long obedience in the same direction." Eugene Peterson saw this truth with such clarity that he titled one of his first books *A Long Obedience in the Same Direction*.

If you're part of a team charged with building your church's ministry to young adults, be prepared for a long drive. This is one of those cross-country family vacations to the Grand Canyon in a minivan kind of journeys. It's no quick trip to the pizza shop.

Any plan to address the complexity of young adult ministry begins with the recognition that epic, sustainable change for churches, for individuals, for organizations—just doesn't happen quickly.

Time *can* be a productive partner in creating the kind of change that lasts, that doesn't run over people in the process, and that's profound enough to navigate resistance and sabotage. When Ministry Architects works with churches to build young adult ministries, we recommend a five-year horizon. Quick fixes—especially in the church—usually are neither quick nor do they fix much of anything.

When working the processes outlined in this book, you'll experience days of rapid growth when enthusiasm is high, when you feel the wind in your sails. Then there will be days when your ministry simmers on the back burner or actually takes a few steps backward.

There will be seasons of profound discovery and (more often) seasons of one failed experiment after another. And there will be days —likely many more days—when you just put one faithful foot in front of the other. And on each of those days, you do what needs to be done, working the long, slow process of creating the kind of change that takes root.

When churches are in a hurry to solve the problem of young adult ministry quickly, they're most vulnerable to the kind of classic mistakes that, in the long run, require immensely *more* time. Hurried churches tend to launch a series of herky-jerky initiatives, assuming that a single home-run solution is the answer. Or they focus on single, short-lived, isolated events, claiming success way too prematurely.

Your church doesn't have to live that narrative.

Here's what we've discovered: faithful failing in the right direction almost always works. We call it "dumb persistence." This key value has guided Ministry Architects from the very beginning. And it all starts with the words "I don't know . . . yet."

Young adults are by definition a highly diverse, individualistic, and paradoxical people group. As I hope we've proven throughout the past fourteen chapters, you can't build a thriving ministry by imposing a few well-meaning programs on young adults. You must start with a stance of intentional ignorance, which is a pretty good place to begin when working with any new group.

Of course, every church's approach must be, at some level, unique. But at the same time, we're convinced that every church can build a thriving young adult ministry by working the same, deliberate, long-term strategy outlined in this chapter.

One Step at a Time

To borrow from Eugene Peterson's title, I propose that people responsible for launching a young adult ministry practice an "obedience" to a basic process, to a system that, when practiced over time, is almost certain to guarantee results. I'm not saying this is the *only* process that works—only that you need a process. Use ours. Use someone else's. Create your own system. But work a deliberate plan.

Don't make the rookie mistake of cobbling together a few isolated "great ideas" from books, seminars, and ministry anecdotes and expect them to work. They won't, at least not for the long haul.

Though previous chapters have touched on various components of this system, the following is a step-by-step process your church can use as a road map to get started (the appendix contains an expanded Young Adult Ministry Road Map).

Step 1. Assess the landscape. The first step focuses on evaluating resources, with eyes wide open to the kind of effort and investment this project requires. You'll ask, realistically, "How valuable is this ministry in the landscape of everything else our church does?"

* *Determine whether building a young adult ministry is worth it.* Because launching a ministry requires a long-term, sustained investment of time, volunteers, and resources, good stewardship requires counting the cost. Every church considering this question should ask, "Are we willing to invest time, energy, and focus over the next five years to build a ministry that effectively engages, disciples, and dispatches young adults into mission?"

Though a negative answer may seem heartless, it's far better to never begin than to waste time and resources on work that will be abandoned after the first dozen failures, when church finances get tight, or as committee membership rotates.

* *Take stock of available resources.* Once your church decides to enter the long-launch process, you'll want to identify and compile your resources:

  ○ Develop a database (contact list) of any and all young adults connected to your church, even distant connections. Remember: this isn't a list of just the young adults who would identify themselves as members or attendees of your church. It must include the barista you've gotten to know at your favorite coffee shop and the son of a church member who's serving overseas.

  ○ A good rule of thumb is that you're ready to begin inviting young adults to "programming" only after you have a database list of fifty or so young adults.

  ○ Create a database of local resources that connect to young adults in the community. This can include local colleges, other churches, restaurants, coffee shops, and apartment complexes that draw young adults.

- o Develop a list of any potential volunteers in the church who might have a heart and a vision for building a thriving young adult ministry, including young adults themselves.

- o If you have young adult programming that's working, compile a one-page calendar and description of those programs, including the number and names of young adults involved.

Step 2. Gather and equip a team. Don't try to go alone into unchartered territory. Invite and prepare a team of fellow travelers to go along.

* *Pray for young adults.* Even before your first team meeting, get into the habit of praying by name for the young adults in your community (using the aforementioned database as a prayer guide). Once your team is recruited, invite them to establish the same practice themselves. Nothing focuses a team on the specific needs of your young adults quite like praying for them.

* Build a team. Your team can be as small as three members or as large as ten. In a perfect world, at least one-third of the team will be young adults themselves, but don't let an inability to hit this target stop you from moving forward. The key is to have a team, with each person's role always including building a relationship with at least one young adult not yet on the team. (A sample job description and meeting agenda for this team are online at ivpress .com/sustainable-young-adult-ministry.)

- o *Warning*: As you start to build a team, you don't want a highly anxious, impatient, easy-answer person who will cry "The sky is falling!" at the first steep hill. Here's a clue: if a potential team member tends to use the word *just* a lot (e.g., "We just need to get a class started"), you likely have the wrong person.

- ○ The most important team member will be someone (perhaps two someones) willing to champion this effort for at least the next five years. It isn't necessary to expect every team member to make a five-year commitment, but it's wise to have the project's champion work with a five-year horizon.

- ○ In addition to the point person(s), you'll need to cover the following skills, understanding that one team member may have more than one of these:
  - database management and tracking
  - entrepreneurship
  - marketing and social media
  - local mission
  - volunteer development
  - leadership role in the church (from which to effectively advocate for and communicate about young adult ministry)

* *Get outside support.* The team should determine whether it needs to accelerate and ensure progress by including a consulting group with a focus on young adult ministry (e.g., ministryarchitects.com or another group with a similar young adult focus). Though this may seem like an extravagance, consider this comparison: few churches would consider a major capital campaign without a campaign consultant. Few churches would consider a major building project without an outside firm to help. When it comes to accomplishing a mission your church has never successfully completed before, it can save a lot of time and money to have someone on your team who knows the process and has already completed it successfully.

* *Anchor your team in reality.* Your first meetings as a team involve anchoring it in the real world of young adult ministry. Most

people will come to this mission with some idea of how it "should" be done, usually based on little more than their experiences with youth or young adults themselves. Most conveniently forget the fundamental reality that almost *all* churches are, by their own estimation, failing in this area of ministry.

It will be natural to begin with easy-answer suggestions such as, "All we need to do is what Young Life, a popular campus ministry, is doing." To counter this tendency, work this training process:

- o Confirm the job description for the Young Adult Ministry Team, updating it as necessary.

- o Do a group study of this book together (using the discussion questions at the end of this book). To avoid getting bogged down, have your team complete this study in three months or less, if possible (but no more than six months).

- o Identify a few churches with *similar demographics* as yours that are doing *something* right in their young adult ministry. Do a case study of each church to identify any transferrable principles. Note: if you're a 150-member, hundred-year-old mainline church, it likely won't help to benchmark against the 2,000-member, ten-year-old church across town that has catered to young adults from day one!

Step 3. Engage young adults' first fruits. Now that you and your team have a clear view of what you have and where you want to go, the next step is to gather the low-hanging fruit by creating easy access points for the young adults you've been meeting or who are already within your team's orbit.

- * *Deliberately build connections.* This step ensures that your work with young adults comes from your relationships *with* them rather than great ideas *about* them.

- Remind the group that the most important part of their work is getting to know specific young adults in the church and community.

- Create a master list of all the young adults who team members are connected to in some way, including who's connected to whom.

- This is the point when team members begin tracking and recording the relationships they're each building with young adults, a process that happens at every Young Adult Ministry Team meeting (see "Young Adult Intentional Relationship Plan Tracking Sheet" at ivpress.com/sustainable-young-adult-ministry).

✱ *Select a young-adult-friendly mission.* Find one local mission effort in your church that you can immediately begin inviting young adults to. An ideal mission includes the following characteristics:

- Ease of involvement (e.g., multiple scheduling options, no lengthy training requirements, proximity to the church).

- Already a strong connection with your church, with multiple champions for this mission within the congregation.

- A mission that resonates with a wide spectrum of young adults.

- A turnkey project that lets people show up, get oriented, and begin working without having to collect and transport lots of tools and supplies.

- If your church doesn't have a local mission project that fits, you'll need to find (or create) one.

- Create a calendar of mission-engagement opportunities for young adults for the coming year, with at least one event per quarter.

* *Promote, engage, and track young adults.* Once your mission is set, develop easy-entry opportunities for young adults to serve in it.

- o Invite young adults in your database to make a difference in the community, encouraging them to bring friends who might enjoy being part of this kind of mission experience. This can happen through email or social media, but—especially early on—you'll want to ask each young adult directly.

- o For each project or event, have a team of non-young adults and young adults in more or less equal number.

- o When the group gathers for the project, take a few minutes to introduce the volunteers to one another and gather contact information for any new person serving.

- o As the work progresses, ensure there's ample space for relational connections during the project or during meals afterward so non-young adults can take initiative to learn about each young adult.

- o Add into the young adult database the contact information for new participants, track the participation of attendees, and include appropriate notes (e.g., "new to town," "mom is a pastor," "working in the music business").

- o Stay connected through social media or email with all young adults who participate in a mission project, continually updating them with progress reports and opportunities to participate again.

- o Continue improving and expanding this process until your team feels comfortably connected with at least ten young adults. For some churches, this can easily take a year or more.

Step 4. Listen and discern your next-step model. Now that you've built relationships with young adults and have begun engaging some of them in an outward-focused mission, it's time to discern their particular passions for innovating, leading, and impacting the world around them.

* *Listen to their change-the-world dreams.* By this point in the process, your team will have built relationships with quite a number of young adults who have, at one time or another, been involved in your mission. It's likely that a few of them may have become part of the life of your church.

   Now's the time to be more intentional about listening to people's change-the-world dreams in order to position them to begin leading the next step of ministry together.

   Just to clarify: When I say, "Listen to their dreams," I'm not suggesting you give them a survey and ask what young adult programs they'd like the church to offer! This step involves spending quality time in conversation with young adults— as individuals and in small groups—to discover what issues make their hearts beat faster and what challenges in the church and world they're passionate about solving.

   You're listening for a unique call that God may be stirring in them. Some will be happy to be part of a change-the-world enterprise—either the church's or someone else's. But a few will have dreams that may never come to fruition without the support and colaboring of a church such as yours.

   What you're bringing to the conversation is a desire to help people discern and shape those dreams into something that can become a reality. Remember, at this point you haven't launched anything. You're still just listening.

* *Discern your next-step model.* The exact expression of young adult ministry can, eventually, take many forms. But we recommend at this point that you choose one of these two foundational models, each designed to put young adults in the driver's seat.

o Option 1. Build your own change laboratory. This option
allows young adults to help shape and incubate change in the
church or community. Here you're creating a space to listen
to, develop, and implement specific ideas for change fueled
by the passions of your young adults. Those ideas for change
might come in the form of a social enterprise to address a
community need or in the form of an innovation to change
how the church does its work.

The whole point of the laboratory is for young adults to
start from a stance of being partners in the church's mission
rather than recipients of its programs. The laboratory provides a collaborative space for experimentation (and failure)
as young adults work with the support of other generations in
implementing positive change initiatives. (See a sample plan
at "Change-the-World Missional Laboratory Launch Plan"
online at ivpress.com/sustainable-young-adult-ministry.)

o Option 2. Launch a one-year intensive program in Christian
leadership. The untethered season of young adulthood
provides an open door for the church to offer targeted,
trajectory-setting leadership development for the next generation. During these years of transition, many young adults
will be enthusiastic about the chance to sink their teeth into
a defined leadership-development process, network with
people outside their generation, and build their résumé all at
the same time.

The one-year intensive program varies from an "everyone is welcome" Bible study or class. It's a high-commitment small group focused on preparing young adults for Christian leadership, especially
those who *won't* go into ministry vocations. And there's a good
chance that at least some of these young adults will have a desire to
experience leadership within the life of the church. (See "Sample

Launch Plan for a Next Generation Leadership Academy" for a general outline and structure for launching a Young Leaders Academy. See "Case Study for Next Generation Leadership Academy" for how our friend Chris Sasser led such a program. Both can be found online at ivpress.com/sustainable-young-adult-ministry.)

Step 5. Sustain and build engagement. As you engage young adults in one of these two foundational models, *they* very well may develop their own Bible studies or fellowship groups. When they do, celebrate!

Just don't confuse these groups with the heart of your young adult ministry. They can be energizing *byproducts*, but the laboratory and the leadership institute models provide ongoing fuel for young adult engagement.

In addition, you can continue inviting new young adults into your young adult-friendly mission activities. One key to sustaining a thriving ministry is to continue to invite, track, and connect with young adults who aren't already part of your ministry.

To ensure continued momentum, you can add these habits into the ongoing rhythm of your ministry with the understanding that you first want to complete the four *building* steps without spending lots of energy on these *sustaining* steps:

* *Establish regular launching rituals.* Understanding the highly transitional nature of young adult life, engage your congregation in celebrating these transitions. Create regular rhythms and rituals that commission and send young adults into new mission wherever they're heading.

* *Build a multigenerational culture.* By now, your team should no longer be the only members of your church's older generation who are caring for and investing in young adults' lives. Continue inviting, thanking, and telling the stories of older adults connecting with the younger generation.

* *Respond to their leading.* Young adults themselves will come up with programming they find meaningful in the church. They may start a supper club, a Bible study, a new worship service, a new mission, or a community-wide young adult initiative. They may push for more generationally diverse leadership. The church should welcome these ideas even though many of them might be (and sometimes should be) short-lived.

* *Create short-term discipleship experiences.* Invite young adults into discipleship opportunities with follow-up reunions. This can be a three-week topical study, a cultural-immersion mission experience, a discipleship-oriented adventure trip, and the like. Build several of these into the next twelve-month calendar and provide appropriate promotion, invitation, and follow-up.

* *Create regular communication rhythms.* Throughout the process, continue to build your database and regularly communicate with your young adult audience about opportunities for service together. Be sure to use communication methods that are *most applicable* to the generation you're reaching. Group email blasts are okay for reminders to people who've committed to participating in a particular event, but they're almost useless in getting new people to attend.

Beyond Running in Circles

Did you know it's almost impossible for a human being to walk in a straight line for any period of time? It's true. Psychologists actually documented this by performing a set of simple experiments.

They asked a few volunteers to walk in a straight line for as long as possible. Some walked through a flat, forested region of Germany, others through the Sahara Desert in Tunisia. Both places were vast and without visible landmarks in the distance. After a few hours of walking, they checked the GPS trackers.

The results show that the walkers *always* ended up walking in circles, no matter how hard they tried to walk a straight line. One researcher noted, "Just walking in a straight line seems like such a simple and natural thing to do, but if you think about it, it's quite (a) complicated thing going on in the brain."[1]

Later, they repeated the experiment but blindfolded the participants. This variation resulted in *more* circle-walking in even smaller, tighter circles.

It's just natural for humans—and churches—to walk in circles. Though it might seem simple, building a ministry, especially a new one such as young adult ministry, often makes us circle the familiar territory of repeated mistakes, unable to set a course toward breakthrough change.

This chapter's landmarks will prevent you from going in circles. If you follow this process, you'll move forward, one step at a time, in the same direction. Take the list of landmarks and focus on moving toward the very next one. The pace isn't the issue; the direction is what matters. It's not a sprint but a marathon. To borrow Peterson's title again, it's a "*long* obedience in the *same* direction."

Failure Isn't an Option—It's a Certainty

*Now is not the time to wave the white flag. Actually,
just the opposite. Now is the time to aggressively embrace
and empower a generation that will be next to carry the baton.*

TONY MORGAN

Vires acquirit eundo.
(We gather strength as we go.)

VIRGIL

I n the year 2000, a little file-sharing website called Napster turned the music industry on its ear. A year later, Apple introduced the first-generation iPod, offering the capacity to put "a thousand songs in your pocket." And now, countless iterations later, digital media downloads for music, movies, TV shows, and books have become, far and away, a standard method of consuming media.

Now it's normal. But it's a new normal compared to 1999 and before.

Maybe you remember the days when the new digital landscape was just opening up, a world where everyone could copy music and share it without cost. This new arrangement offered a wide-open door for music distribution and, on the flip side, for widespread pirating and theft of copyrighted intellectual property.

Lawsuits were filed, and Napster lost a court battle with the Recording Industry Association of America. Napster eventually filed for bankruptcy, and the music industry breathed a sigh of relief, thinking, "At least *that's* over!"

After the brief unpleasantness, the world of commercial music could go back to its previous method of distributing music and movies the way God intended—through CDs and DVDs.

Not so much.

Though Napster burned brightly and quickly and lost in the courts, it forever changed the industry. A door was opened that could never be closed, and the entire recording business had a choice to make.

Leaders could wring their hands, make doomsday predictions, and long for simpler times, or they could reinvent their work based on the new reality. Now, less than two decades after Napster's death, the folks left standing in the music industry are, by and large, those who shifted into the new reality. They learned to live, and even thrive, in the new digital age.

Maybe the church can learn a lesson or two from Napster about navigating disruptive change.

Every church has a choice. We can cling to the ministry models and methods fit for a church that no longer exists, models and methods we've grown comfortable with for decades if not centuries. Or we can open ourselves to the possibility of the Spirit's prompting in and through the disruption, prompting us to reinvent our churches in ways congruent with the new world before us.

If it feels as if the questions being raised by color-outside-the-lines young adults have the potential to unhinge the church, it's because, by the grace of God, they do.

The Cost of Change

There is, of course, a downside to embracing this paradoxical approach to young adult ministry, apart from the long, persistent work required.

Because young adult ministry is, by definition, innovative, and because innovation itself can be messy and disruptive, this process can't help but create a little (maybe even a lot) of institutional resistance among people who hold the keys to church leadership.

I was fascinated to learn recently of a theory developed by a ministry friend. His name is Doug, so he calls it "Doug's Law," just in case it catches on. It states:

Meetings required to make a decision = church's age ÷ 10

Stated simply, Doug's Law holds that the number of meetings required to make a single decision in your church is directly proportionate to the number of decades your church has been around.

For example, if your church is less than ten years old, most decisions get made without having a single meeting. If it's fifty years old, that same decision can require as many as five separate meetings with various teams, committees, or individuals. And if your church is one hundred years old or more, according to Doug, may God have mercy on your weary soul!

If you're in an established church, you know how notoriously difficult it can be to successfully launch new things. You know the institutional inertia that relentlessly sucks good ideas back into the gravitational pull of its core, where movement seldom occurs.

As a result, if your church chooses to create a new focus on young adult ministry, it will—if done right—almost inevitably cause a stir and require *many* extra meetings. It may make people uncomfortable. It may result in underground resistance and sabotage. It may give rise to irrational institutional roadblocks.

You can be sure that no matter how much initial support the idea of young adult ministry has, it *will* cost something. I'm not saying your church must give up its beloved worship style. I'm not saying you'll have to rip out the pews and put in a coffee bar or get a younger pastor in the pulpit every now and then. (I'm not *not* saying those things either.)

I'm saying that unless you're a new church with a laser focus on young adults already, the shift toward creating a thriving young adult ministry requires managing sometimes-complex change.

And change naturally creates resistance.

At some level, you'll be asking hard-working, deeply invested leaders to step back a bit and allow young adults, new to the party, to share the leadership load. You'll be asking veteran volunteers to share power with young adults, knowing there's a good chance the younger generation will be more likely to fumble the ball.

You'll be asking long-term members who've always seen the church as a place of respite, a place filled with people like themselves, to widen their circle to include a twenty-something (or two) who looks, thinks, and acts more than a little different from them.

You'll be asking leaders to hand over a few keys to the church, knowing that those who receive them may not value the church in the exact same ways as those who built it.

Pastors have lost their jobs over less.

Read those last few paragraphs again and you'll get an idea why it's so easy, so natural for churches to stay stuck in a regressive status quo, wondering why there aren't more people "like us" showing up.

This dynamic, perhaps more than any other, is the root cause of the most disturbing trend identified in chapter one: most churches aren't even *trying* to reach young adults.

The good news, despite this reality check, is that young adult ministry isn't only possible, but it has the potential to bring a flood of new missional vitality into your church. First, you must be prepared enough to continue slogging through the seasons when this ministry is an uphill climb.

The Slow Road to Rapid Change

We've seen churches snap like dry twigs under the weight of the unbridled enthusiasm of people passionate about their pet projects. Impatience can cause zealous folks to unwittingly sabotage their own change efforts.

If you've been around the church a few years, you've likely witnessed a church body being split in two, not because a change initiative was ill-conceived but because the rollout was.

Bend wood at too sharp an angle, too quickly, and it will splinter and snap.

But under the right conditions and with enough patience, wood can be bent, twisted, and turned in almost any direction.

This kind of change takes slow, deliberate pressure in a sustained direction. It takes time to create systems that produce the kind of change that both energizes *and* lasts.

Secrets of Sustaining Change

One Saturday afternoon, my father and I tackled a garage project—repairing a broken ladder from my bunk bed. The steps were in place, but only one side rail was usable. It was going to be a quick job. All we needed to do was cut the wood to replicate the existing side rail, and we'd be done in less than an hour (or so we thought).

After cutting the first new rail, we realized we should've cut a mirror image of the existing rail, not an exact replica. So we tried again.

For the second attempt, we got the mirror image right but cut the slots for the steps at the wrong angle. And the third time wasn't a charm because we cut the slots at a different but still wrong angle.

By the fourth try, our quick project had devolved into a frustrating afternoon of arguing, finger pointing, and cold silence.

The typical church tries to solve the young adult problem as a quick and simple project. It invests little in the way of design and immediately gets to work, making one mistake after another, cutting and recutting, frustrated that the wood isn't cooperating.

Maybe it's time for the church to step back from the hurry-up crisis language surrounding young adult ministry. Maybe it's time to begin working with a set of blueprints that can be implemented one step at a time.

As you and your team enter the process of moving young adult ministry from a marginal aspiration to a core mission of your church, here are a few words of caution to help you slow down to just the right pace:

1. *The process works (if we work the process).* You might have picked up this book for a variety of reasons. One of the most common we've heard is that readers have already tried everything they can think of, but nothing seems to have worked. By now you know this book isn't designed to give you a new idea; it's designed to help you get off the roller coaster of ideas and into a steady, sustainable process for success.

My coauthor, Mark, is known to say, "We don't need great ideas in ministry. We just need to operationalize the lousy ideas we already have." We've observed that when the processes outlined in this book don't work, the problem usually isn't with the process. It's because we stop working the process and rely instead on shortcuts and simplistic solutions such as events, personality, or a single, silver-bullet program.

The process of building a constellation of relationships beneath a young adult ministry can feel too slow for many impatient champions. Tapping into young adult passion for changing the world has many more layers and steps than simply throwing out a young adult Bible study and promoting it.

When (not if) you and your team get stuck, return again to the process (summarized in chapter fifteen) and work it.

2. Not all nos are created equal. When (not if) you hear a no from the powers that be in your congregation (or from the young adults themselves), remember that negative responses and resistance are simply a natural part of progress. Some nos are born out of fear or a lack of information. Some are born out of personal hurt. Some come from past failures. And some provide the very information we need to create a better plan.

Before you throw up your hands assuming nothing will ever change, stay committed to keep knocking. When you continue bringing up the right questions with the right spirit on a regular basis over a span of years, the walls of resistance almost always crumble. Churches that give up on their young adult ministry at the first sign of resistance will never have the kind of effect they desire.

3. Dumb persistence is your friend. As you begin the implementation process, it won't be long before you come up against a question or a challenge you simply don't have a solution for. The great news is you don't need all the answers to begin the journey.

Martin Luther King Jr. was right: "Take the first step in faith. You don't have to see the whole staircase, just take the first step."[1] Many of the people we respect the most in ministry made some of their most profound contributions when they had no money and were doing what they had never done before.

Roadblocks are an absolutely predictable part of this process. If you find yourself restarting parts of it again and again until you get some traction, you're right on track. This is normal. You are normal.

When you're stuck, keep going. There is incredible power in just taking the next single step, even when you don't know how you'll solve the next problem.

4. Persistence requires a champion. Proverbs 29:18 offers a one-sentence clinic in leadership: "Where there is no vision, the people perish" (KJV). And where there is no champion for the vision, everyone forgets it.

For a young adult ministry to launch sustainably, someone must carry the banner. Someone has to champion the cause. A group of helpers, all leaning on each other, won't get the job done. Someone needs to own the role of champion. Whether that's a volunteer, a staff member, or even the senior pastor, the champion wakes up most mornings thinking about the next person to engage, the next problem to solve, the next message to share in young adult ministry.

5. Patience is a virtue. By now, I hope it's clear that the process we've outlined is a slow one. For many churches, just getting a team to connect with young adults and build a database of contact information takes months. This process is designed to be worked one step at a time rather than with all the plates spinning at once.

If you work this process well, you'll naturally be impatient, particularly at first. When you are, consider yourself right on track!

Too often, church life is driven by the urgency of the moment, so we react rather than build something with a long-term impact. Church life is *busy*. Life is busy. Our natural inclination is to leap from one thing to the next in an attempt to put out fires (or sometimes even starting them).

Ours is a slow-roast recipe for success, not fast food. If you're feeling anxiety that not enough is happening as you work this process, take a great lesson from our friends in recovery and repeat after me, "One day at a time."

Lasting Little Latin Lesson

I recently came across a Latin phrase that sums up our hope for how you'll implement this book's principles: *Solvitur ambulando.*

Literally, it translates, "It is solved by walking"—or, more loosely, "We'll find the answer while we're moving."

Every step of the work we're called to do with the next generation can't be mapped out. We'll set a clear course and work out many of the details along the way.

In a recent Harvard University study, Bill Sahlman found, "Business plans rank no more than a 2—on a scale of 1 to 10—as a predictor of a new venture's success." And often the more detailed the plan, the more likely it is to flop.[2] As far back as 2002, it was revealed that of companies in the list of America's 500 fastest-growing companies, only 40 percent wrote formal business plans and two-thirds of *those* eventually ditched their plans. A study of the clients of Endeavor, a coaching company for startups, revealed that two-thirds of their clients didn't write business plans, and 50 percent changed their business model at least once.[3]

More often than not, successful companies, churches, and families practice that Latin proverb, "We'll find the answer while we're moving." As you build your young adult ministry, look for people with resilience, people with the ability to keep *moving* in the same direction, despite the obstacles.

Project Friendship

After spending time with his disciples, Jesus makes an important distinction: "I no longer call you servants [but] friends" (John 15:15). *Friends* here might mean more than you think at first glance.

Today we use *friend* in a wide variety of ways, referring to a pal, a BFF, someone in your group, or even someone who just makes you laugh when you're together. Jesus' group of friends included people who would have been mortal enemies in "the real world."

A zealot passionate about overthrowing the Romans and a Roman tax collector would have found themselves on opposite sides of almost every issue. But in Jesus, two diametrically opposing sides come together as friends.

One way to see the process outlined in this book is as a systematic way of building a constellation of friends between people in generations that are often divided. We're excited to provide a way of seeing over the wall to where the other lives.

Fundamentally, this work we're being called into is a partnership with the God who brings together the likes of zealots and tax collectors, senior citizens and young adults, insiders and outsiders— all united as friends around the Spirit and the gospel that sends us out together.

So take a step back, take a deep breath, fasten your seatbelt, and decide whether you'll be part of this epic work of turning strangers into friends.

Acknowledgments

Scott

I'm so thankful to the following people who've made this book possible:

Cindy, my wife, who holds an unwavering belief that some of my ideas are actually good ones.

Rock Harbor Church, who taught me everything I know about working with young adults.

Pastors Tom Elenbaas, Tim Wilson, Greg VanderMeer, Tanner Smith, and all my friends at Harbor Churches who've provided opportunity and passion to work with young adults in our churches and who've been willing to try, fail, and repeat with enthusiasm!

Doug McClintic, who astutely developed "Doug's Law" and showed me what it feels like when an older generation successfully equips a younger one.

Jeff Dunn-Rankin, a young adult at heart, who ate BBQ in Texas with me and got it into my head that we could actually help churches reach young adults.

Chris Sasser, for actually doing so many of the things in this book (and making them work).

Those young adults who provided stories or statements for this book: Chelsea, Jordan, Michael, Louis, Gabe, Zach, Carol, Lexi, Malorie, and Ryan.

Katie Kuatz, Jordan Stonehouse, Matt Kooman, Chelsea Van-Noord, and Chris Thompson, who all contributed to the creation of the workbook.

Mark DeVries, who not only made my words sound like something a human would say but provided the wisdom, know-how, and encouragement to make this project a reality.

Mark

I'm so grateful for our team at Ministry Architects, particularly my coauthor, Scott Pontier, for working to develop systems that actually help ordinary churches engage young adults in a sustainable way.

My young adult children, Adam and Sara, Debbie and Trey, and Leigh have fueled my passion for helping ordinary churches have thriving, magnetic ministries with a generation untethered. You've been my best conversation partners and most lively co-conspirators in this venture.

The bold, creative, unconventional young adult ministry staff at First Presbyterian Church in Nashville inspires me every week. Ashley and Josh, thanks for continuing to try things no one expects to work and doing what's needed to make them succeed.

Our conversations with partners, editors, and contributors are too numerous to mention. But I want to express particular gratitude to Laura Addis, Debbie Freeman, and Leigh DeVries, who each contributed to this project in invaluable ways.

Our digital communications guru, Barry Hill, helped us find ways to unconventionally distribute this project to ensure that this primer won't be our last word on the subject but the first prototype in a series of clarifying and expanding iterations. The Moose is loose!

Our Ministry Architects churches have provided us with the greatest dojos in the world to practice our craft. If this resource has the impact we're dreaming it will, it's thanks to your unwavering commitment to move us beyond theory to practices that produce lasting fruit.

And finally, of course, Susan, the bride who married me when we were barely young adults ourselves. You're the smartest, most hilarious member of our family. Whatever is beautiful, noble, and holy in our young adult children, I blame it all on you.

Discussion Questions

Introduction

1. This book was written as a conversation. Who would you like to invite into the conversation by reading this book and discussing it with you?

2. Do a quick assessment of your church's efforts at young adult ministry. What has worked? What hasn't? What worked for a little while but no longer does?

3. Take an inventory of the experience you bring to the table, either as someone who's tried to lead a young adult ministry or someone who's been thinking of starting one.

Chapter 1: How Do You Solve a Problem Like Young Adults?

1. What do you know or what have you heard about young adults and the church?

2. How would you describe the current state of affairs when it comes to your church's efforts at young adult ministry?

3. What has been normal in your own ministry context in conversations about young adults?

4. After being introduced to the six mistakes, which one surprises you the most?

5. Which mistakes have been the most common in your congregation?

6. Of all the statistics you read in this chapter, which, if any, surprises you and why?

Chapter 2: Mistake 1

1. Which of the five traditional markers of adulthood still apply to young adults today?

2. Which of those markers seem irrelevant to this particular generation of young adults?

3. Do you have any personal examples of the lengthening adolescence, whether for you, a family member, or a friend?

4. Name all the young adults you know personally.

5. How many young adults would you guess the average leader at your church knows personally?

6. What has your church already done to get to know young adults better?

Chapter 3: Mistake 2

1. What attempts has your church made to attract young adults to attend?

2. If your church has experimented with a different worship experience or style in order to engage young adults, what have been the results?

3. Do an inventory of your church's weekly worship experiences. What about those experiences might be attractive to a typical young adult, and what might repel them?

4. In your worship services, what's the average age of the people in upfront leadership?

5. Assuming that your church wants more young adults to attend worship, what changes do you think the church would be willing to make? What changes are off-limits?

Chapter 4: Mistake 3

1. This chapter suggests it's a mistake to add young adult ministry to a youth director's list of responsibilities. In what ways do you agree? In what ways do you disagree?

2. How would your church define *success* for its young adult ministry?

3. Review the statistics from the Sticky Faith research. What is surprising about these findings?

4. How have you seen these findings proven or contradicted in your congregation?

5. What is your model for reaching young adults, and how closely does it resemble your model for reaching teenagers?

6. In what ways is it essential that the approaches for youth ministry and young adult ministry are distinctly different?

Chapter 5: Mistake 4

1. List the programming options your church has tried for young adults. What has worked well? What hasn't worked so well?

2. What have been the long-term results of your church's young adult program?

3. What opportunities has your church created for young adults to intentionally interact with the larger congregation?

4. What programs has your church created for young adults that separate them from other generations in the church?

5. Would you say your church's focus is more on activating young adults for mission or getting them to attend some program?

Chapter 6: Mistake 5

1 If young adults in your congregation were interested in taking on a leadership role, what path would they have to take? How difficult would that path be for them to find?

2. Who are the young leaders you know in and around your congregation?

3. What strategy does your church have for apprenticing young leaders?

4. What young adults do you know who are leading in the world around you?

5. What would have to change to give young adults more access to decision-making and leadership in your church?

Chapter 7: Mistake 6

1. What might cause your congregation to give up on the vision of developing a thriving young adult ministry?

2. Who are the people in your church who won't give up on young adult ministry?

3. Taken as a whole, how would you rate the level of hopefulness among your church's leadership about building a sustainable ministry to young adults? (10 = We can do this! 1 = The end is nigh!)

4. What obstacles stand in the way of your church making young adult ministry a priority right now?

5. Write an imaginary "Debbie Downer" list of reasons why young adult ministry will *never* work in your church.

Chapter 8: Beyond Fixing

1. This chapter says fixing mistakes isn't enough. Do you agree?

2. From this chapter, what makes you most excited? What makes you most hesitant?

3. This chapter sets out the six paradoxes to building ministry with young adults. Which one seems to be the easiest for your church to accomplish? What would be your first step?

4. Which one feels the closest to impossible? Why?

Chapter 9: Paradox 1

1. Where have you seen young adults do something new or creative to make the world a better place?

2. When was the last time your church launched a new ministry initiative?

3. In your church, what's the general response to risk taking?

4. What problems exist in your community that young adults might be passionate about solving?

5. Which people in your congregation might be inspired by the opportunity to partner with young adults in developing creative solutions to a local problem?

Chapter 10: Paradox 2

1. What "impulsive purchase" in young adult ministry might you or your church be tempted to make?

2. What young adult programs have you tried that have been met with less-than-desirable results?

3. What mission opportunities is your congregation currently engaged in that could be natural to invite young adults into?

4. What young adults could be champions for a particular mission the church currently engages in?

5. What missions besides those your church currently supports seem like the most organic fit for the young adults you know?

Chapter 11: Paradox 3

1. When you were a young adult, what older adults helped shape your identity and how?

2. In what ways has your church engaged (or failed to engage) older generations in ministry with young adults?

3. Why do older generations in your church avoid engaging with young adults?

4. Can you name any examples of older adults who've already effectively built relationships with young adults?

5. Who in your church are the most likely candidates for being part of your young adult ministry team?

Chapter 12: Paradox 4

1. After this introduction to systems thinking, what questions or wonderings do you have?

2. As you look through the list of systems, which, if any, are already in place for your church's work with young adults?

3. In what ways does a systems approach match your church's culture? In what ways does it look totally different?

4. If your team could start working on a single system today, which do you think would have the greatest impact?

5. What is the biggest obstacle your team faces in building the essential systems of a sustainable young adult ministry?

Chapter 13: Paradox 5

1. To what kinds of activities do you see young adults in your community committing to sacrificially?

2. In what ways has your church tried to engage young adults by lowering the bar for their commitment?

3. What young adults do you know who would respond well to the challenge to a new level of ministry engagement or responsibility?

4. Where in your church's ministry might a young adult take on a significant leadership role?

5. If your church were to launch a more high-commitment opportunity for young adults, what might it look like? Which three young adults would be your first-round draft picks?

Chapter 14: Paradox 6

1. Have you witnessed any seasons of transition in your church's ministry with young adults in the past?

2. What, if anything, does your church currently do to celebrate young adult transitions?

3. What are some ways you can celebrate young people's transitions and label them as a "sending" instead of a "losing"?

4. What small cohort of young adults can you gather in this season?

5. What initiatives can you develop to regularly, personally, and creatively invite new young adults into your church community?

Chapter 15: I Don't Know . . . Yet

1. Tell about something you're glad you stuck with despite discouragement and doubt. What happened?

2. In the process of thinking about and developing a healthy young adult ministry, when have you already been discouraged?

3. Where is your church's ministry in the steps listed in this chapter? Did you miss any that you need to go back and pay attention to?

4. Which step feels the most challenging for you and your team right now? Why?

5. Who on your team is willing to commit the next five years to the process of building a thriving young adult ministry in your church?

Chapter 16: Failure Isn't an Option—It's a Certainty

1. As you reach the end of this book, how do you feel about the task before you?

2. How comfortable are you with the prospect of failing forward with your young adult ministry?

3. On a scale of 1 to 10, how resilient is your young adult ministry team?

4. How might you seek and engage the support of your church's senior leadership for this project?

5. If Scott and Mark were in your group, what questions would you have for them? (If you really want to know what they'd say, feel free to email them: scott@ministryarchitects .com, mark@ministryarchitects.com)

Appendix

The Young Adult Ministry Road Map

T his road map attempts to put into summary form the essential steps for building a thriving young adult ministry in your unique context. Whether you're renovating an existing ministry or starting from scratch, the road map can reorient you along the journey when you're lost or wandering.

The road map provides clarity about your long-term destination and where you're specifically heading on the journey's next phase. When you need more detail about the terrain of a particular leg, you can return to the book. But this road map provides a clear overview of landmarks along the way—and steps you'll need to take.

It will be tempting to skip over the foundational stages and jump right into planning programs. Most normal young adult ministries use this approach, and most achieve abysmal results. Some of this work will be a trial-and-error, experimental process. When things don't work as planned, celebrate what you've learned and try something new. Nothing works until it does!

Stage 1: Prepare for the Journey

* Create an older-generation database.

   o key players and partners

- helpers and cheerleaders
- anyone else in the church with a heart for engaging the next generation

* Create a young adult database.
  - currently in the church
  - currently out of town
  - currently in town but not in the church

* Take inventory.
  - current effective young adult ministry programming
  - current calendar for young adult ministry

Stage 2: Engage Your Traveling Companions

* Identify the roles you'll need on the young adult ministry team.
* Recruit a team of partners and key players.
* Gather the team for orientation to clarify roles.
* Schedule regular team meetings.
* Identify a point leader for your church's young adult ministry initiative.
* As soon as possible, invite young adults who share a passion for young adult ministry to serve in meaningful roles on the team.

Stage 3: Learn the Landscape

* Become fluent in the world of young adult ministry (working through this and other books).
* Establish a process for getting to know specific young adults in your church and community.
* Work the process of getting to know specific young adults in your church and community.
* List all the places in your community that influence young adults.

* Establish habits of continuing to build relationships and make connections with young adults who aren't yet part of your church.

Stage 4: Try a Few Excursions

* Identify a young adult-friendly mission to invite young adults to participate in.

* Engage an approximately equal number of young adults and older adults in your first short-term (two- to four-hour) mission excursion.

* Based on the first prototype excursion, schedule additional mission excursions.

Stage 5: Pack Your Bags

* Develop basic control documents for your young adult ministry.

  o an updated database

  o a missional calendar for the next twelve months

  o an updated website with all pertinent information about your young adult ministry

  o a communications game plan, including social media (for an example see "Communication Game Plan" online at ivpress .com/sustainable-young-adult-ministry).

  o a master list of possible leadership roles in which young adults can serve in your church

  o a budget for the young adult ministry for the coming year

  o a volunteer recruitment and training process (for an example see "Volunteer Recruitment and Training" online at ivpress .com/sustainable-young-adult-ministry).

  o a job description for each of your young adult ministry staff and volunteers, if necessary (for an example see "Ministry Job Descriptions" at ivpress.com/sustainable-young-adult-ministry).

- ○ a preventive maintenance calendar to ensure that your leadership team regularly tends to fundamental systems required to keep the ministry healthy (for an example see "Preventive Maintenance Calendar" at ivpress.com/sustainable -young-adult-ministry).

- ○ a game plan for celebrating rites of passage for sending young adults into new phases of life and new ministry opportunities (for an example see "Creating a Sending Culture and Launching Rituals" at ivpress.com/sustainable-young-adult-ministry).

- ○ a young adult ministry manual that includes all the above documents

* Draft visioning documents for your young adult ministry.

- ○ mission statement

- ○ tagline

- ○ core values

- ○ three-year measurable goals with one-year benchmarks

- ○ an organizational chart

Note. At this point, you haven't formally invited a single young adult to attend your church or to participate in a young adult class or small group. You've simply partnered with them in missional experiences and worked to build collaborative friendships between young adults and other generations. Should young adults choose to develop a class, Bible study, or mission project, the Young Adult Ministry Team will support the efforts of young adults launching and guiding these programs themselves.

As a general rule, wait to offer traditional young adult programming until you have at least ten regularly connected young adults engaged and at least fifty young adults in your database. If you aren't at this point yet, don't proceed to step 6 (where most failing ministries try to begin). Instead, go back through the previous steps, continuing to build more relationships with young adults and to invite them more regularly into missional excursions.

Step 6: Plan Your Trip

* Draft a plan for developing young leaders for your church.

* In collaboration with young adults, determine your program offerings for next year.

* Create an informal laboratory for incubating the missional dreams of young adults.

* Draft a plan for infusing your church with an intentionally intergenerational DNA.

Step 7: Launch Your Journey

* Launch the first prototype to implement your game plan for developing young leaders.

* Launch the first prototype for incubating the missional dreams of young adults.

* Launch the first prototype of placing young adults into specific church-leadership positions.

* Launch the first prototype designed to infuse your church with an intentionally intergenerational DNA.

Step 8: Sustain and Improve the Journey

* Iterate and improve your game plan for developing young leaders.

* Iterate and improve your game plan for incubating the missional dreams of young adults.

* Iterate and improve your game plan for placing young adults into specific church-leadership positions.

* Iterate and improve your game plan for infusing your church with an intentionally intergenerational DNA. This includes short-term equipping opportunities.

Notes

1 How Do You Solve a Problem Like Young Adults?

[1]David Kinnaman and Aly Hawkins, *You Lost Me: Why Young Christians Are Leaving Church—and Rethinking Faith* (Grand Rapids: Baker, 2011).

[2]Cathy Lynn Grossman, "Young Adults Aren't Sticking with Church," *USA Today*, August 6, 2007, http://usatoday30.usatoday.com/news/religion/2007-08-06-church-dropouts_N.htm.

[3]"Most Twentysomethings Put Christianity on the Shelf Following Spiritually Active Teen Years," Barna, September 11, 2006. Retrieved September 9, 2015, https://www.barna.com/research/most-twentysomethings-put-christianity-on-the-shelf-following-spiritually-active-teen-years.

[4]Amelia Thomson-Deveaux, "Rise of the Nones," *American Prospect*, 2013, September 19, 2013, http://prospect.org/article/rise-"nones".

[5]"'Nones' on the Rise," Pew Research Center, October 9, 2012, www.pewforum.org/2012/10/09/nones-on-the-rise.

[6]Michael Lipka, "Millennials Increasingly Are Driving Growth of 'Nones,'" Pew Research Center, May 12, 2015, www.pewresearch.org/fact-tank/2015/05/12/millennials-increasingly-are-driving-growth-of-nones.

[7]Kinnaman, *You Lost Me*, 37.

[8]A private conversation Mark had with an anonymous associate pastor.

[9]See "United Church of Christ Young Adult Study" online at ivpress.com/sustainable-young-adult-ministry.

[10]Robert Wuthnow, *After the Baby Boomers: How Twenty- And Thirty-Somethings Are Shaping the Future of American Religion* (Princeton, NJ: Princeton University Press, 2010), 31.

2 Mistake 1

[1]Kelly Williams Brown, "Millennials—Why Are They the Worst?" TedxSalem, January 31, 2014, www.youtube.com/watch?v=ygBfwgnijlk.

[2]"How Millennials Really ARE Different," *Discovery News*, August 8, 2013, www.seeker.com/how-millennials-really-are-different-1767686733.html.

[3]Robin Marantz Henig, "What Is It About 20-Somethings?" *New York Times*, August 21 2010, www.nytimes.com/2010/08/22/magazine/22Adulthood -t.html.

[4]Samantha Raphelson, "Getting Some 'Me' Time: Why Millennials Are So Individualistic," *NPR*, October 14, 2014, www.npr.org/2014/10/14 /352979540/getting-some-me-time-why-millennials-are-so-individualistic.

[5]Henig, "What Is It About 20-Somethings?"

[6]"Most Twentysomethings Put Christianity on the Shelf Following Spiritually Active Teen Years," Barna Group, September 11, 2006, www.barna .com/research/most-twentysomethings-put-christianity-on-the-shelf -following-spiritually-active-teen-years.

3 Mistake 2

[1]Rachel Sloan, "What Millennials Don't Want from the Church," *Baptist News Global*, October 23, 2013, https://baptistnews.com/article/what -millennials-don-t-want-from-the-church.

[2]Rachel Held Evans, "Why Millennials Are Leaving the Church," *Belief* (blog), July 27, 2013, http://religion.blogs.cnn.com/2013/07/27/why -millennials-are-leaving-the-church.

[3]Brett McKracken, "How to Keep Millennials in the Church? Let's Keep Church Un-cool," *OnFaith*, July 31, 2013, www.onfaith.co/onfaith /2013/07/31/how-to-keep-millennials-in-the-church-lets-keep-church -un-cool?noredirect=on.

[4]Rebecca VanDoodewaard, "Young Evangelicals Are Getting High," *Christian Pundit*, July 17, 2013, http://thechristianpundit.org/2013/07/17 /young-evangelicals-are-getting-high.

4 Mistake 3

[1]"'Extreme Cheapskate' Mom Rations Food to Toddlers," *ET*, November 20, 2013, www.etonline.com/tv/141031_Extreme_Cheapskate _Mom_Rations_Food_to_Toddlers.

[2]"What Is Sticky Faith?" Fuller Youth Institute, accessed September 9, 2015, http://stickyfaith.org/family/about/press.

[3]"Most Twentysomethings Put Christianity on the Shelf Following Spiritually Active Teen Years," Barna Group, September 11, 2006, www.barna.com/research/most-twentysomethings-put-christianity-on-the-shelf-following-spiritually-active-teen-years.

5 Mistake 4

[1]"David Kinnaman Is Wrong: How the Church Really Lost the Millennials and What We Can Do to Keep The Next Generation," *The Gospel Side*, September 17, 2013, http://archive.is/ytMbW.

[2]Rachel Sloan, "What Millennials Don't Want from the Church," *Baptist News Global*, October 23, 2013, https://baptistnews.com/article/what-millennials-don-t-want-from-the-church.

[3]Jen Hatmaker, *For the Love: Fighting for Grace in a World of Impossible Standards* (Nashville: Thomas Nelson, 2015), loc. 1257, Kindle.

[4]"Social Change Impact Report," Walden University, accessed November 10, 2015, www.waldenu.edu/-/media/walden/files/about-walden/scir/2014/scir-2014-executive-summary.pdf.

[5]Gabe Lyons, *The Next Christians: The Good News About the End of Christian America* (New York: Doubleday Religion, 2010), 53.

6 Mistake 5

[1]David Greene, "Older Farmers Seem to Be in No Hurry to Call It Quits," *NPR Morning Edition*, August 20, 2013.

[2]Tim Woda, "Kids Can Use Smartphones Before They Learn to Write Their Names," *UknowKids*, February 20, 2014, http://resources.uknowkids.com/blog/kids-can-use-smartphones-before-they-learn-to-write-their-names.

[3]F. Kitto, *YouthWorker Journal*, May 1, 2001, 18-19.

[4]Larry Osborne, *Sticky Teams: Keeping Your Leadership Team and Staff on the Same Page* (Grand Rapids: Zondervan, 2010), 114.

[5]Osborne, *Sticky Teams*, 114.

[6]Naomi Ko, "Flaky Youth, Flaky Future," *Huffington Post*, September 26, 2012, www.huffingtonpost.com/naomi-ko/flaky-youth-flaky-future_b_1784660.html.

7 Mistake 6

[1]Heidi Glenn, "Losing Our Religion: The Growth of the 'Nones,'" *NPR*, January 13, 2013, www.npr.org/sections/thetwo-way/2013/01/14 /169164840/losing-our-religion-the-growth-of-the-nones.

[2]Michael Lipka, "Millennials Increasingly Are Driving Growth of 'Nones,'" Pew Research Center, May 12, 2015, www.pewresearch.org/fact-tank /2015/05/12/millennials-increasingly-are-driving-growth-of-nones.

[3]Trevor Neilson, "Philanthropy and Millennials: Get on Board or Get Left Behind," *Huffington Post*, August 6, 2013, www.huffingtonpost.com /trevor-neilson/philanthrop-and-millennia_b_3269238.html.

[4]Neil Howe and William Strauss, *Millennials Rising: The Next Great Generation* (New York: Vintage Books, 2000), 4.

[5]Thom S. Rainer, "Millennials, Religion, and a Reason for Hope," *Tom S. Rainer* (blog), February 7, 2011, http://thomrainer.com/2012/02/07 /millennials_and_a_reason_for_hope.

8 Beyond Fixing

[1]Haydn Shaw, "Why What You Read About Millennials Seems Contradictory," *Huffington Post*, updated March 15, 2015, www.huffingtonpost .com/haydn-shaw/why-what-you-read-about-m_b_6459946.html; emphasis added.

[2]H. Richard Niebuhr, *Christ and Culture* (New York: HarperCollins, 1951), 157.

[3]Brad Lomenick, *The Catalyst Leader: 8 Essentials for Becoming a Change Maker* (Nashville: Thomas Nelson, 2013), loc 1090, Kindle.

9 Paradox 1

[1]See "United Church of Christ Young Adult Study" online at ivpress.com /sustainable-young-adult-ministry.

[2]Brad Lomenick, *The Catalyst Leader: 8 Essentials for Becoming a Change Maker* (Nashville: Thomas Nelson, 2013), loc. 516, Kindle.

[3]Henrik Bresman and Vinika D. Rao, "Millennials Want to Lead. Are They Ready?" *Forbes*, November 18, 2014, www.forbes.com/sites/insead /2014/11/18/millennials-want-to-lead-are-they-ready.

[4]Sean Graber, "Engaging Millennials Through Leadership Development," Virtuali and New Leaders Council, accessed August 7, 2017, https://

docplayer.net/65296968-Engaging-millennials-through-leadership
-development.html.

[5]Josh Bersin, "Millennials Will Soon Rule the World: But How Will They
Lead?" *Forbes*, September 12, 2013, www.forbes.com/sites/joshbersin
/2013/09/12/millenials-will-soon-rule-the-world-but-how-will-they
-lead/#7796e609227a.

[6]John Ford, "62% of Millennials Believe Themselves to Be Innovative: Are
They Wrong?" *Mic Daily*, February 6, 2013, http://mic.com/articles
/24973/62-of-millennials-believe-themselves-to-be-innovative-are-they
-wrong.

[7]Ford, "62% of Millennials Believe Themselves to Be Innovative."

[8]Kristina Bravo, "10 Cool Products Invented by Millennials," *TakePart*,
October 16, 2014, www.takepart.com/photos/10-coolest-socially-relevant
-products/index.html

[9]Bravo, "10 Cool Products."

[10]Sherri R. Greenburg, "Using Innovation and Technology to Improve City
Services," accessed November 8, 2016, www.businessofgovernment
.org/report/using-innovation-and-technology-improve-city-services.

[11]"Student Startup Creates Online Medical Records for Pets," *Hack Reactor*,
July 11, 2014, www.hackreactor.com/blog/student-startup-brings
-online-medical-records-to-pets.

10 Paradox 2

[1]Larissa Faw, "Millennials Expect More Than Good Products, Services
to Win Their Loyalty," *Forbes*, May 22, 2014, www.forbes.com/sites
/larissafaw/2014/05/22/millennials-expect-more-than-good-products
-services-to-win-their-loyalty/#3449d8a25697.

[2]Faw, "Millennials Expect More Than Good Products, Services to Win
Their Loyalty."

[3]Dave Gilboa, "How Warby Parker's Social Mission Has Attracted Millennials," *Fortune*, January 19, 2015 http://fortune.com/video/2015/06/19
/how-warby-parkers-social-mission-has-attracted-millennials.

[4]Michael Frost and Alan Hirsch, *The Faith of Leap: Embracing a Theology
of Risk, Adventure and Courage* (Grand Rapids: Baker, 2011), 159.

11 Paradox 3

[1]Andrea Atkins, "Six Most Dangerous Sports for Kids," *Considerable*, May 1, 2013, https://considerable.com/most-dangerous-sports-for-kids.

[2]Though only men were permitted to be Levites, this pattern for the transfer of leadership should be seen in today's church as applying equally to men and women in leadership.

[3]Ninety-four percent of the millennials indicate that to some degree they have great respect for older generations (Thom S. Rainer and Jess Rainer, *The Millennials: Connecting to America's Largest Generation* [Nashville: B&H, 2011], 88).

[4]Brad Lomenick, *The Catalyst Leader: 8 Essentials for Becoming a Change Maker* (Nashville: Thomas Nelson, 2013), loc. 2914, Kindle.

[5]Drew Dyck, "Millennials Need a Bigger God, Not a Hipper Pastor," *Aspen Group*, January 24, 2018, www.aspengroup.com/blog/millennials-need-a-bigger-god-not-hipper-pastor.

[6]A. Allan Martin and Clint Jenkin, "Engaging Adventist Millennials: A Church That Embraces Relationships," *Ministry*, May 1, 2014, www.ministrymagazine.org/archive/2014/05/engaging-adventist-millennials.

[7]"5 Reasons Millennials Stay Connected to Church," Barna Group, accessed September 14, 2015, www.barna.com/research/5-reasons-millennials-stay-connected-to-church.

12 Paradox 4

[1]Mark Devries, *Sustainable Youth Ministry: Why Most Youth Ministry Doesn't Last and What Your Church Can Do About It* (Downers Grove, IL: InterVarsity Press, 2008), 51-52.

13 Paradox 5

[1]Lauren Cash, "Generation Flaky," *Breath & Nourish*, June 7, 2013, www.breatheandnourish.com/recent-posts/generation-flaky. (Since we wrote this, it appears *Breath & Nourish* has been removed from the Internet!)

[2]Kate Hakala, "There's a Modern Affliction Ruining Our Friendships— and We're All Guilty of It," *Mic*, March 18, 2015, http://mic.com/articles/113138/there-s-a-modern-problem-afflicting-our-friendships-and-it-s-time-to-talk-about-it.

[3]Dan Schawbel, "Who's at Fault for High Gen-Y Turnover?" *Forbes*, November 22, 2011, www.forbes.com/sites/danschawbel/2011/11/22/whos-at-fault-for-high-gen-y-turnover.

[4]Dan Schawbel, "The Cost of Millennial Retention Study," *Millennial Branding*, August 6, 2013, http://millennialbranding.com/2013/cost-millennial-retention-study.

[5]Rieva Lesonsky, "Survey Says: Are Millennial Employees Flakes?" *Huffington Post*, March 19, 2012, www.huffingtonpost.com/2012/03/19/survey-says-are-millennial-employees-flakes_n_1325331.html.

[6]Steven Shattuck, "4 Insights from the 2015 Millennial Impact Report," *Bloomerang*, June 30, 2015, https://bloomerang.co/blog/4-insights-from-the-2015-millennial-impact-report.

14 Paradox 6

[1]Greg Toppo and Paul Overberg, "Census: Americans Are Moving Again," *USA Today*, October 7, 2014, www.usatoday.com/story/news/nation/2013/10/26/americans-moving-again-census/2986963.

[2]David Bancroft Avrick, "How Many People Move Each Year—and Who Are They?" NCPA, accessed September 9, 2015, www.ncpa.co/pdf/2016ce/exhibit-b-how-many-people-move.pdf.

[3]Jeanne Meister, "The Future of Work: Job Hopping Is the 'New Normal' for Millennials," *Forbes*, August 14, 2012, www.forbes.com/sites/jeannemeister/2012/08/14/job-hopping-is-the-new-normal-for-millennials-three-ways-to-prevent-a-human-resource-nightmare/#7fd568725508.

[4]Reggie McNeal, *This Present Future: Six Tough Questions for the Church* (San Francisco: Jossey-Bass, 2003), 115.

[5]Stephen W. Sorenson, "Moving Targets: Ministry in a Transient Society," *Christianity Today*, accessed September 9, 2015, www.christianitytoday.com/le/1991/fall/91l4120.html.

[6]Lonny Kocina, "The Average American Is Exposed to . . ." Media Relations Agency, February 22, 2006, www.publicity.com/advicetips/the-average-american-is-exposed-to.

[7]Francis I, "I Prefer a Church Which Is Bruised, Hurting and Dirty," *USA Today*, November 26, 2013, www.usatoday.com/story/news/world/2013/11/26/pope-francis-poverty/3759005.

[8]Michael Duduit, "Reaching the Millennials: An Interview with Thom Rainer," *Preaching*, December 5, 2011, www.preaching.com/resources /articles/11660599.

[9]Duduit, "Reaching the Millennials."

[10]Keith Miller and Bruce Larson, *The Edge of Adventure* (Tarrytown, NY: Fleming H. Revell, 1991), 36.

15 I Don't Know . . . Yet

[1]Jan Souman, quoted in Emily Sohn, "Turns Out, Lost People Really Do Walk in Circles," *NBCNews*, August 20, 2009, www.nbcnews.com /id/32494981/ns/technology_and_science-science/t/turns-out-lost -people-really-do-walk-circles.

16 Failure Isn't an Option—It's a Certainty

[1]Martin Luther King Jr., "I Have a Dream," in *Let Nobody Turn Us Around: Voices of Resistance, Reform, and Renewal: An African American Anthology*, ed. Manning Marable and Leith Mullings (Lanham, MD: Rowman & Littlefield, 1999).

[2]Linda Rottenberg, *Crazy Is a Compliment: The Power of Zigging when Everyone Else Zags* (New York: Penguin, 2016), 39.

[3]Rottenberg, *Crazy Is a Compliment*, 37.

Additional Resources

The following additional resources are available for free online at ivpress.com/sustainable-young-adult-ministry.

* Sample Launch Plan for a Next Generation Leadership Academy
* Ministry Job Descriptions
* Creating a Sending Culture and Launching Rituals
* United Church of Christ Young Adult Study
* Change-the-World Missional Laboratory Launch Plan
* Case Study for Next Generation Leadership Academy
* Young Adult Intentional Relationship Plan Tracking Sheet
* Volunteer Recruitment and Training
* Preventive Maintenance Calendar
* Communication Game Plan
* Meeting Agenda Template for a Young Adult Ministry Team

MINISTRY ARCHITECTS

Helping Churches Create
Sustainable Change

There tends to be two very different types of people in ministry. The first focuses on systems, structures, and stability. The end result of their work is stability. The second is a disruptive innovator, one who brings energy, creativity, and a whirlwind of passion to a ministry.

Stability can quickly turn into sterility, and energetic change initiatives are often short-lived, personality-driven, and have a tendency to leave a path of disruption and instability in their wake.

There is a better way. The church needs both:

○ healthy systems

○ inspiring, catalytic innovation

The church needs sustainable change; change that sticks.

At Ministry Architects, we help churches navigate the challenging journey through change. We help you build the systems that ensure stability without sacrificing creativity and innovation. Change that lasts.

We are a team of experienced pastors, children's ministers, youth workers, and professors who provide coaching for ministry professionals and consult with churches and ministry teams to create sustainable change.

To find out how we can help you lead sustainable change in your church or ministry, contact us at

info@ministryarchitects.com
877-462-5718

This book also entitles you to take our Children's Ministry Diagnostic absolutely free. You can do so at

diagnostics.ministryarchitects.com
use the passcode SCMye4hu